a healing marriage

a healing marriage

biblical help for overcoming childhood sexual abuse

brad and cheryl tuggle

NAVPRESS®

BRINGING TRUTH TO LIFE

OUR GUARANTEE TO YOU

We believe so strongly in the message of our books that we are making this quality guarantee to you. If for any reason you are disappointed with the content of this book, return the title page to us with your name and address and we will refund to you the list price of the book. To help us serve you better, please briefly describe why you were disappointed. Mail your refund request to: NavPress, P.O. Box 35002, Colorado Springs, CO 80935.

The Navigators is an international Christian organization. Our mission is to reach, disciple, and equip people to know Christ and to make Him known through successive generations. We envision multitudes of diverse people in the United States and every other nation who have a passionate love for Christ, live a lifestyle of sharing Christ's love, and multiply spiritual laborers among those without Christ.

NavPress is the publishing ministry of The Navigators. NavPress publications help believers learn biblical truth and apply what they learn to their lives and ministries. Our mission is to stimulate spiritual formation among our readers.

ISBN 1-57683-602-9

Cover design by David Carlson Design
Cover photo by Corbis
Creative Team: Jay Howver, Arvid Wallen, Steve Parolini, Cara Iverson, Glynese Northam

Some of the anecdotal illustrations in this book are true to life and are included with the permission of the persons involved. All other illustrations are composites of real situations, and any resemblance to people living or dead is coincidental.

Unless otherwise identified, all Scripture quotations in this publication are taken from the HOLY BIBLE: NEW INTERNATIONAL VERSION® (NIV®). Copyright © 1973, 1978, 1984 by International Bible Society. Used by permission of Zondervan Publishing House. All rights reserved. Other versions used include: THE MESSAGE (MSG). Copyright © 1993, 1994, 1995, 1996, 2000, 2001, 2002. Used by permission of NavPress Publishing Group; the International Children's Bible, New Century Version (NCV), © 1983, 1986, 1988 by Word Publishing, Dallas, Texas 75039. Used by permission; the New King James Version (NKJV). Copyright © 1982 by Thomas Nelson, Inc. Used by permission. All rights reserved; and the New American Standard Bible (NASB), © The Lockman Foundation 1960, 1962, 1963, 1968, 1971, 1972, 1973, 1975, 1977, 1995.

Tuggle, Brad, 1959-
  A healing marriage : biblical help for overcoming childhood sexual abuse / Brad and Cheryl Tuggle.
    p. cm.
  Includes bibliographical references.
  ISBN 1-57683-602-9
  1. Marriage--Religious aspects--Christianity. 2. Child sexual abuse--Religious aspects--Christianity.
I. Tuggle, Cheryl. II. Title.
  BV835.T84 2004
  248.8'44--dc22
                        2004008446

Printed in the United States of America

1 2 3 4 5 6 7 8 9 10 / 08 07 06 05 04

FOR A FREE CATALOG OF
NAVPRESS BOOKS & BIBLE STUDIES,
CALL 1-800-366-7788 (USA)
OR 1-416-499-4615 (CANADA)

contents

preface

I do not think that all who choose wrong roads perish; but their rescue consists in being put back on the right road. A wrong sum can
be put right: but only by going back till you find the error and working it afresh from that point, never by simply *going on*. Evil can be
undone, but it cannot "develop" into good. Time does not heal it.

— C. S. LEWIS, *The Great Divorce*

You know how someone can tell you something, maybe let you
in on a secret, but it's not until a long time later — perhaps
years — that you begin to understand the weight of what you were
told? That's the way it was when Cheryl and I first met. In the early
stages of a relationship, much of the conversation is about the past.
You chat about where you were born, where you went to school, how
big your family is, and so on. When Cheryl and I started dating years
ago, it didn't take long to learn she was still recovering from her
divorce a few months earlier, she wasn't close to her family, and she
didn't have a big circle of friends. It took a little longer — about a
month into our relationship — to find out she had grown up in an
abusive home. It took longer still to uncover the painful truth that this
included not only physical abuse but also sexual abuse.

I wish I could tell you that realization led me to a new level of compassion for Cheryl. I wish I could tell you I responded in a way that honored her struggle and drew us closer together. I wish I could tell you I even understood what was meant by *sexual abuse*. I can't.

My faith in God wasn't a big help either. Even though I had been a believer since childhood, I had no idea how to respond. Even though Cheryl started coming to church with me, we didn't know what to do. How do you ask for help with something like this in *church*, of all places? Even when she trusted Christ and was baptized, we didn't know how to process this or how to tell anyone at church about our struggles. Four months after she became a Christian, we married. Sitting in church on Sundays and Wednesdays, we were newly-weds — and emotional strangers. We were trying to build a life together without the faintest clue how years of sexual and physical abuse were affecting us. We had no idea of the baggage brought into our relationship because of that treatment. We were completely ignorant of how far apart we were, much less what to do about it.

Since then, we have met countless people just like us: couples more concerned with maintaining a facade of "normal" for the outside world than with admitting their fear of connecting with others; couples who recognized they had a problem but didn't know why; couples who were more emotionally intimate with casual friends than with each other; couples whose physical intimacy was a matter of duty, an act to be endured, or a weapon for leverage.

To this day, we deal with the ripples (some days, the tidal waves) caused by the effects of sexual abuse. Every day we have to re-decide to show grace and not resentment, mercy and not judgment, and take intentional steps toward each other rather than retreat. Our desire in this book is to give the encouragement and counsel we were so desperate for when we met. We want to build a safe harbor for Christian couples working through the lifelong impact of childhood sexual abuse.

Our pasts have been catalysts to conflict, misunderstanding, and sin in all areas of our lives: our personal walk with God, our marriage relationship, our role as parents, and our conduct as members of the body of Christ. Our experience has taught us that C. S. Lewis was right: Our marriage could not have been patched up, glossed over, therapeutically diagnosed, or made whole *without* going back and retracing our steps to see where the problems originated. Then, and only then, could we start reworking our relationship *from there*, using God-designed navigational charts to get us back on track.

But it had to begin, as Lewis suggested, with a fresh start. We had to begin our journey at a place of surrender. Without recognition of our own inability to solve the problem, our capacity to move toward true relational health — true marriage community — would have been impossible.

It's sometimes hard to see past injuries and failures, but this is the redemption Jesus came to bring: a forgiveness of grievances, a release of injustices, and a partnership in restoration that can bring the emotional, spiritual, and physical fulfillment God designed for all of us. We live in a world stained by sin, but healing is possible.

This book has been written to both you and your spouse. You are in it together. The book begins with two letters: one to the survivor and one to the spouse. Interspersed throughout each chapter are "Pause and Reflect" sections designed to facilitate dialogue as you work through your understanding and perspective of the past. This may be difficult at first, especially if you've never been able to talk about your abuse, the humiliation and shame, and how it made you feel. Many of the questions in these sections are for only the survivor, but it would be helpful for the spouse also to read those questions and reflect on them from the other's perspective.

Your responses and your spouse's responses to the issues, letters, Scriptures, and questions will probably be very different. You will likely move through the material at different speeds. Because of this, we recommend that each of you have your own copy of the book to record responses, highlight meaningful sections, and note areas that speak specifically to your situation. When you do share with each other, we hope you can see something of your own struggle in ours, and we pray you would gain wisdom from God's Word as He lays out a blueprint for your relationship.

Please also note we have used female pronouns when referring to abuse survivors, and male pronouns when speaking of the spouse. This is not to suggest sexual abuse of males is not a significant issue but is to reflect that the overwhelming statistical majority of abuse victims are female.

This book may be a first step for you. Maybe you're wondering which, if any, of the issues in your marriage might be traced back to an abusive environment. If you've never talked about your abuse, perhaps the mere presence of this book in your home can be an icebreaker for discussing the subject. Please keep in mind, though, that initial disclosure of an abusive past, if done in an abrupt and unexpected way, can be difficult for a spouse to hear and respond to. If you are a survivor and are considering broaching this subject for the first time with your spouse, you might want to consult with a professional counselor first. This could help you determine whether or not the timing is right for disclosure, as well as the best way to proceed.

There was no road map for the first several years of our journey, but we pray that by revealing our struggles, misunderstandings, and victories, we can communicate a message of hope to couples who badly need it.

In the end, it is the admission of our own helplessness and our reach to understand the astonishing love of Christ that will empower His Spirit to heal us. This has been our prayer for you. We prayed for you before you read this, even before the book was written. May God grant each of us humility of heart to grasp the width, height, and depth of His love.

a letter to survivors

ear Friend,

We are sorry. We're sorry you're a fellow traveler on the road from past sexual abuse. We hurt with you, and we are praying for you.

Maybe you've never been able to talk about how you were sexually abused as a child or teenager. Maybe you've felt too ashamed to tell anyone. Perhaps you tried to open up once or twice, but the people you trusted dismissed what you said. Maybe they told you to "just get over it" or criticized your faith and reprimanded you for not forgiving and forgetting.

If you come from a Christian home, you might have endured tremendous tension by living with a parent or sibling who seemed a Christian by day but was a predator by night. Perhaps at church you concealed who you were, lest someone learn the truth about you and surely reject you all over again.

We are sorry for what happened to you, for how much it hurt, and for the burden you carry today because you were forced to be someone's plaything. We're sorry you feel alone and isolated. We're sorry you may have felt, and perhaps still do feel, responsible for what happened to you. For the first of many times in this book, let us stop and say: It was *not* your fault.

You were manipulated. You were seduced, and *no one* had the right to mastermind a scheme to exploit you for his or her own obscene pleasure. It was wrong — *they* were wrong.

We know that you're tired. You're worn out from pretending you live a perfectly normal life. You're exhausted from having to keep everything in order. You're tired of feeling like you always have to apologize. You're weary of expending so much energy working to solve everyone else's problems. You're spent from constantly being on guard against people who seem kind or gentle. This suspicion goes against your better judgment, but you believe there's no way you can risk giving in to intimacy or vulnerability. Still, keeping everybody at arm's length wears you out.

You've probably asked yourself many questions over the years:

- What really happened?
- What if I can't remember everything but can recall only a few images or a few seconds of mental videotape? Can I really be sure anything happened?
- Why am I still consumed by this so many years later?
- Does my abusive past contribute to the "disconnectedness" I feel between my husband and me?
- Isn't it best just to turn off my sexuality? All it's ever done is hurt me.
- I don't know the difference between right and wrong feelings of intimacy. What do they look like?
- I remember that sometimes it hurt, but sometimes I felt pleasure. Didn't I really deserve what happened if it felt good?
- Where was God when I was being abused? Is He as disgusted with me today as I am with myself?

You were the victim of someone else's sin. In a strange way, it's easier to blame yourself than to put the responsibility where it belongs. But once again, it was *not* your fault. Shame and guilt may have helped you cope with the enormity of the offense, but they are Satan's tools to keep you in bondage to your past. You were the victim of a crime. If someone shot you because of your proximity to a robbery, you might suffer injury for the rest of your life because of the crime. Your presence at that location, at that time, would not be a reason for you to feel guilty. The guilt belongs to the perpetrator.

Perhaps you wanted desperately to be loved, even by your perpetrator, and would have done anything for attention. Maybe you were starved for affection and didn't flee those situations even though they made you uncomfortable. There is nothing wrong with wanting to be loved — that is a God-given desire. But does that mean you are somewhat responsible for the abuse?

No, you aren't. If carbon monoxide secretly leaked into your office or home, would you somehow be culpable for getting sick or passing out? Of course not. Your environment was poisoned, and Satan, well aware of our God-driven need to inhale the warmth of acceptance and esteem, made you believe those feelings are toxic. You were callously and deliberately used. If the Enemy succeeds in convincing you to permanently close off your feelings — to hold yourself responsible for someone else's depravity — he has won an important battle. Do *not* give in to this lie!

In wartime, rescued prisoners of war are often moved into a program called *decompression*. Decompression is a mental healing process in which psychologists help ex-POWs normalize the mental adjustments they had to make in order to cope with isolation, degradation, and being under the total control of someone else. They help ex-POWs deal with feelings of survivor guilt, depersonalization, grieving for lost time and ruined relationships, and other results of their imprisonment.

As a survivor of sexual abuse, you were stripped of your personhood, not unlike a POW. You were robbed of your childhood and your identity because you were made to feel you existed only to satisfy someone else's needs. The vulnerability you felt *then* carries into *today*, and you probably have found ways to control your environment so you *never* feel that helpless again.

We want to help you decompress. We are praying that you can take steps toward the God who is perfectly trustworthy — in whose arms you can finally exhale, rest, and feel safe. Doesn't that sound good? Doesn't the prospect of being able to finally unclench your fists, relax your shoulders, and let down your guard a little sound attractive?

With God's help, you can. That may seem scary, but it's the way to a freedom you've always wanted but never had, a release from fear designed just for you before the foundation of the world. Don't worry — God will meet you right where you are.

We know He will meet you, because that's exactly what Jesus did. He became man precisely to meet us in our humanity, accepting people where He found them: hurting, confused, angry, sorry, and sinful. He became human to experience what it's like to be *you*. As a survivor of abuse, wounded and humiliated, you, of all people, understand the shame Jesus endured. And He completely understands your suffering. In a significant way, you and Jesus share a bond of common experience. He understands how it feels to suffer the consequences of someone else's sin, to feel alone in the darkness. He knows what it's like to be desperate for hope, pleading for deliverance, naked, exposed, and in pain. He completely understands the torment of silence in the midst of abuse. He is the One who offers you hope:

> "Are you tired? Worn out? Burned out on religion? Come to me. Get away with me and you'll recover your life. I'll show you how to take a real rest. Walk with me and work with me — watch how I do it. Learn the unforced rhythms of grace. I won't lay anything heavy or ill-fitting on you. Keep company with me and you'll learn to live freely and lightly." (Matthew 11:28-30, MSG)

Jesus came to earth, lived, and died to sympathize with you, and He rose again to give you hope. His victory is your victory, a triumph all believers will celebrate with Him personally and permanently. It's not time for that celebration yet, but it's coming. There is hope. We will walk with you in search of that hope, and we will pray for your spouse to walk along with you as well.

Your friends,
Brad and Cheryl

a letter to spouses

Dear Friend,

Whether you've just now found out you're married to an abuse survivor or you've been trying to deal with that fact for some time, it's probably safe to say you've already gotten much more than you bargained for.

As the spouse of a survivor, it's hard for you to listen to horrific stories about the pain endured by someone you love and at the same time feel powerless to do anything about it. Your natural inclination is to protect your wife and shield her from harm. Yet trying to deal with her abuse is like fighting blindfolded without a weapon.

You're frustrated and even angry because:

- You are unjustly dealing with the effects of someone else's sin.
- You feel ambushed by emotions you had no part in producing.
- You live in an atmosphere of constant uncertainty.
- You can't understand how consistent behavior on your part can produce totally unpredictable behavior on hers.
- You have an overwhelming desire to "turn back the clock" and undo the damage.

You may also be confused if your spouse exhibits:

- Extreme difficulty in making a decision ("Whatever you want is fine with me.")

- Obsessive attention to appearance (unwillingness to go out, too much modesty in dressing or undressing, anxiety about weight changes)
- The inability to receive compliments ("Stop teasing me!")

In my relationship with Cheryl, these things drove me crazy. So what did I do? I fell back on my strength: I became Mr. Fix-It. I analyzed the problem, developed a foolproof process to deal with the contingencies, and then attempted to implement it. Something needed to be done, and we weren't going to fail for lack of trying! I wanted desperately to fix what was broken; the problem was, I didn't know what needed fixing.

I now understand that Cheryl didn't need me to fix *anything*. My terrific problem-solving skills were of no use here. Perhaps the most significant thing I learned as the spouse of a survivor is this: It's not about what you can *do*; it's about who you can *be*. It's not about doing; it's about being — being supportive, being open enough to ask how you can serve, and just *being there*.

The aftereffects of sexual abuse are many and varied. You might wonder why your spouse didn't just tell someone. You might speculate that something could have been done *if only* someone had known what was going on. Couldn't telling a parent or family member have produced swift action, immediate protection, and expedited prosecution?

Most survivors (perhaps even your own spouse) will tell you that if they somehow found the courage to tell someone what was happening, they were dismissed, ignored, or criticized. They may still, years later, be held in contempt by family and friends for telling the truth and destroying the pretense of the "perfect family."

It's not just the family that trivializes or discounts what happened. Almost every abuse victim has heard such phrases as:

- "It happened a long time ago, and you should be over it by now."
- "If your walk with God were where it should be, this would no longer be an issue. You could just forgive and forget."
- "Time should have healed all wounds."

We pray that this book and our experiences will encourage you to listen closely, actively, and empathetically. The extent to which you are able to accept your wife and her story, grieve with her, and reaffirm your love for her will set the tone for your relationship from here forward. It's likely that what you will hear (if you haven't heard it before) will shock, anger, and disgust you. You will be tempted to turn away and ask not to hear more, but it's critical not to tune out or shrink from her story, as difficult as it may be.

As a husband (and a brother in Christ), you can be a significant, powerful component in her healing process. As you have probably seen, virtually every area of your life together is affected by this experience. The importance of your ability to listen and accept the truth about her experience, and your courage to move with her toward wholeness, cannot be underestimated.

One last thought: Remember that God is sovereign. His plans and His timing are perfect. And even though you might feel totally unequipped to deal with this, even though you might feel ambushed or powerless to help, you are precisely where God wants you. In your weakness, God asks you to turn to Him for strength. If you are to serve and minister to your wife, the first step is to reach the point of surrender — to admit you can't do it alone — and ask for God's help.

> We are praying for you.
> Brad and Cheryl

introduction

I t's not something discussed in polite company. It's not something usually shared between friends. It's normally not something disclosed in small-group settings. Many couples that have been married for twenty or thirty years can't discuss it. And it's definitely not talked about in a religious or spiritual context, because, well, it has to do with sex. And it's dirty. And it has to do with the worst kinds of evil that humanity can inflict on itself.

The first step is always the hardest, and you've taken that. You've opened a door to each other — and to God. You've opened a new awareness of each other's viewpoint. You've opened a book about equipping a Christian marriage to deal with childhood sexual abuse.

setting the table

If Cheryl and I had you over for dinner, especially for the first time, we'd do our best to create a pleasant environment in which to spend our evening. We'd clean up the house so you wouldn't trip over our kids' toys; we'd turn on some lights to make the house warm and inviting; we'd put on relaxing background music; and we'd set the table with nice dishes, silverware, and maybe a decoration or two.

That's what we want to do in this book. Already, we've written you letters so you'll know we are fellow travelers on the same road.

Now we will set the table and create an environment that allows us to examine sexual abuse in a spiritual context. We'll try to bring everyone into the same "room" of understanding by reviewing the magnitude of the sexual abuse epidemic and defining terms we'll be using throughout this book. Then we'll "sit down to dinner" and survey a road map from Colossians 3 that will lead us to a number of stops on our journey toward healing.

a spiritual biosphere

Have you ever tried to deal with the effects of your abuse? Perhaps you did so in a clinical counseling setting. Perhaps it was with a support group. Maybe you decided to trust one or two close friends or a sibling with what happened.

It's likely you didn't deal with this in a spiritual climate. Traditionally, sexual abuse, sexual addiction, homosexual feelings, and even substance abuse are taboo topics in Christian circles. And while a growing number of churches are beginning to speak openly and with healing about these issues, few survivors are likely to risk vulnerability in the uncertain landscape of this new area of church ministry. Sadly, church can be the last place that hurting people would be willing to display weakness. It's much easier to put on a mask and pretend to be what we wish we were.

I (Brad) grew up in a church that seemed more concerned with completing "spiritual checklists" than dispensing grace. My level of spirituality and maturity was judged within the church by how many good works I did, how involved I was, and how often I attended services. Later, God helped me see that none of that had anything to do with how much He loved or accepted me. But throughout childhood and into adulthood, the pressure and expectations of the church manifested themselves in one loaded question: "How have you proven yourself this week?"

My church became not a haven of rest but a performance-based organization. Any battles I was fighting or struggles I was enduring had to be purged prior to entry. What I internalized was this: The church did not exist to help me process my anxieties, relieve my burdens, or find rest for my soul.

How much more hopeless and devalued do those of us feel who bring sexual shame to the table? Sexual abuse survivors are often meticulous and unceasing in their attempts to conceal their real selves, *especially* in church. For many people, church is a place where they want to appear the most put-together, in control, and spiritual.

Today's culture is very permissive and blatant about parading sexuality to a public seemingly starved for more. Consequently, churches purposely move away from the subject, fearing contamination and guilt by association. But in doing so, we risk leaving in darkness those who most need dialogue on this topic. We rob them of a vehicle — *the* vehicle, Christ's church — in which to heal, share, and be loved and accepted.

The local church is Christ's community. God works through, and manifests Himself to, His church today. The church is God's biosphere — a protected, cherished hothouse where souls should be lovingly and attentively nourished. Just as a hyperbaric chamber saturates an ailing body with oxygen to stimulate growth and promote healing, so the church must be God's insulated infirmary where survivors are saturated with acceptance and love to enable *spiritual* regeneration.

This book deals with an ugly, messy subject from a Christian perspective. The foundation for our approach will include the following assumptions:

- The one lasting solution to undo this and every other evil is redemption through Jesus Christ.
- Personal faith and obedience to Jesus as Savior is the one relationship that will meet each and every need of all believers.
- The community of this solution, His church, is uniquely designed to "comfort those who are in any affliction" (2 Corinthians 1:4, NASB) with peace from God Himself.
- The greatest earthly extension of that community is the marriage relationship.

In this book, you will read the stories and experience the anxieties and triumphs of survivors. And while all the names have been changed, the facts have not: God has moved powerfully in the lives of these people, and His Spirit is actively healing their self-esteem, relationships, and marriages.

pause & reflect

Pause now and ask God to bless your study together. Specifically pray for courage to communicate honestly with each other, for openness to God's Spirit, and for wisdom in ministering effectively to each other.

the facts

We'll begin by applying a scope and definition to the problem of sexual abuse. Sexual abuse of children is an epidemic. It's estimated that one in four girls is sexually abused before the age of fourteen, and one in six boys is sexually abused before the age of sixteen.[1] And if the local church is a demographic reflection of its neighborhood, the percentages are likely the same inside the church as out.

In this book, we will use the term sexual abuse *survivor* rather than *victim* because the word *survivor* carries with it a sense of hope, endurance, and ultimate victory. We hope that by God's grace you will move beyond survivor and say as Paul did, "In all these things we are *more than conquerors* through him who loved us" (Romans 8:37, emphasis added).

Sexual abuse of children can be defined as "any sexual activity — verbal, visual, or physical — engaged in without consent, which may be emotionally or physically harmful and which exploits a person in order to meet another person's sexual or emotional needs. The person does not consent if he or she cannot reasonably choose to consent or refuse because of age, circumstances, level of understanding, and dependency on or relationship to the offender."[2]

That's a long but somewhat vague definition. What does sexual abuse of a child look like? Specific examples include:

- Showing a child pornographic or revealing pictures
- Exhibitionism (prolonged nudity in front of a child)
- Having a child present during sexual activity
- Having a child inappropriately touch or stimulate an older child or adult
- Talking about or describing nudity or sexual acts to a child
- Touching or fondling in any sexual way, especially breasts or genitals
- Oral sex with a child
- Any vaginal or anal penetration

Keep in mind this is an incomplete list. You may be able to identify some of these examples in your past. But whether or not your experience is listed here, it's important that you try to share it with your spouse at some point during this study. If you're uncomfortable talking about the specifics of your abuse, please don't feel pressured. But to the extent you are able to verbalize and communicate what happened, you can loosen the bondage to those secrets.

pause &
reflect   Spouses, take a moment to reaffirm your commitment to and love for your wife. If you have felt confusion or uncertainty in the past about how to help, share this with her. Pray together and ask God to form you into the servant-husband He designed you to be.

where we're going

Remember Romans 8:37? "In all these things we are more than conquerors through him who loved us." If we are to become more than victims of sexual abuse — more than survivors — our focus must be on our redemption in Christ. This book will focus on a few key verses from the New Testament. One of the most powerful passages that describes our life in Christ is found in Colossians. After outlining the supremacy and authority of Christ and His victory on the cross (Colossians 2), Paul made a plea for holiness (conformity with Christ):

Therefore, as God's chosen people, holy and dearly loved, clothe yourselves with compassion, kindness, humility, gentleness and patience. Bear with each other and forgive whatever grievances you may have against one another. Forgive as the Lord forgave you. And over all these virtues put on love, which binds them all together in perfect unity.

Let the peace of Christ rule in your hearts, since as members of one body you were called to peace. And be thankful. Let the word of Christ dwell in you richly as you teach and admonish one another with all wisdom, and as you sing psalms, hymns and spiritual songs with gratitude in your hearts to God. And whatever you do, whether in word or deed, do it all in the name of the Lord Jesus, giving thanks to God the Father through him. (Colossians 3:12-17)

This passage aligns in a powerful way with five of the most common effects of sexual abuse:

- Shame (verse 12: "Therefore, as God's chosen people, holy and dearly loved . . .")
- Damaged relational intimacy (verses 12-13: "Clothe yourselves with compassion, kindness, humility, gentleness and patience. Bear with each other and forgive whatever grievances you may have against one another. Forgive as the Lord forgave you.")
- Incompleteness (verse 14: "And over all these virtues put on love, which binds them all together in perfect unity.")
- Desire for control (verse 15: "Let the peace of Christ rule in your hearts, since as members of one body you were called to peace. And be thankful.")
- Need for accountability (verse 16: "Let the word of Christ dwell in you richly as you teach and admonish one another with all wisdom, and as you sing psalms, hymns and spiritual songs with gratitude in your hearts to God.")

We will deal with each of these effects in the following chapters.

Colossians 3 is typically not referenced in a marriage context. We have specifically chosen a text outside of that characterization for three reasons. First, we can, and sometimes do, become so accustomed (and almost desensitized) to the passages dealing directly with marriage that they cease to move our hearts and instead evolve into familiar old quotations rather than inspired words of God.

Second, because of the effects of abuse in survivors' lives

(especially problems with control, discussed in chapter 5), passages referencing wives' submission to husbands can be contentious. These Scriptures require significant study and are outside the scope of this book.

Third, and perhaps most significant, we sometimes focus so much on attempting to deal with each other through the lens of how we understand the marriage commands that we lose sight of the far greater host of Scripture that speaks to us as brothers and sisters in Christ. We can gain significant insight by reconsidering the directives to *all* believers, especially in a one-on-one, believer-to-believer, husband-to-wife relationship.

The last chapter deals with an uncomfortable yet critical issue between survivor and spouse: sexual intimacy. While Colossians 3 does not speak to this directly, it's important that any resource dealing with abuse recovery address this issue unflinchingly. We will attempt to discuss the subject directly, with honesty and sensitivity.

It will not be easy, but we have a God who has promised to honor movement toward Him:

> I love those who love me,
>> and those who seek me find me. (Proverbs 8:17)

> Then you will call upon me and come and pray to me, and I will listen to you. You will seek me and find me when you seek me with all your heart. (Jeremiah 29:12-13)

At that time I will deal
>
> with all who oppressed you;

I will rescue the lame

> and gather those who have been scattered.

I will give them praise and honor

> in every land where they were put to shame.

(Zephaniah 3:19)

God will honor the courage you have shown in your willingness to deal with this issue. There is no place we can go that is beyond His love and nothing that His love cannot produce in us. May God bless your work together.

where are we?

Pamela and Alicia are at opposite ends of the same spectrum. Both were sexually abused by their fathers, but that's where the similarities end.

Pamela's marriage lasted almost thirty years; Alicia has lived with a number of men. Pamela is a deeply religious woman whose faith is a cornerstone of her life; Alicia's ability to believe in an all-knowing, loving God ended a long time ago. Pamela controlled and eventually cut off her need for physical intimacy soon after her daughter was born; Alicia has a strong sexual appetite that she desires to feed constantly.

And then there's everyone in between.

In this chapter, we will build a starting point by exploring:

- How we are the same, yet different
- Why we shouldn't compare ourselves or our experiences with others
- How personality issues affect communication
- Where we go from here

First, let's set a biblical benchmark.

two opposite truths

Even a casual reading of the Bible reveals two compelling yet seemingly opposite truths.

truth #1: we are all the same.

The first truth is that we are all the same. We have all been created in the image of God, for the purpose of good, with emotion, intellect, and will. In addition, we all struggle with sin and have the same desperate need for a Savior. As Christians, we are redeemed by a gift of grace and are indebted beyond measure.

As survivors of sexual abuse, we have even *more* in common. We share a damaged sense of self, who we are, and what we were created for; we have a desire to be valued, validated, and heard; and we look at intimacy through a damaged lens.

Many survivors in the support groups we lead come from Christian homes. One of the earliest and most powerful discoveries group members make is that they are not alone. They discover a community of damaged, hurting people in the church who have suffered the same abuse and humiliation. They discover a community of people who know the same guilt and shame and who have also tried to make sense of the unimaginable.

As group members tell their stories of abuse, tears of connection and empathy come from other group members who know exactly what they're talking about and how they feel. They discover they are not alone. They discover that in many ways, they are all the same.

truth #2: we are *not* all the same.

The second truth is that we are each unique. Consider:

Your hands made me and formed me. (Psalm 119:73)

For you created my inmost being;

you knit me together in my mother's womb. . . .

My frame was not hidden from you

when I was made in the secret place.

When I was woven together in the depths of the earth,

your eyes saw my unformed body.

(Psalm 139:13,15-16)

Indeed, the very hairs of your head are all numbered. Don't be

afraid; you are worth more than many sparrows. (Luke 12:7)

Not only are you unique but you are perfectly and completely known by your Creator. He understands your hopes, dreams, and fears. Though He intentionally made you the way you are, His perfect design has been damaged and hurt by sin. But take heart! God has a plan despite this, a purpose He has planned for you since the foundation of the world:

For we are God's workmanship, created in Christ Jesus to do

good works, which God prepared in advance for us to do.

(Ephesians 2:10)

The following is part of Cheryl's story. It might be much the same as yours, or it might be very different. We hope that if you haven't yet been able to talk about what happened, you will take encouragement from her account and step out to share your past in a trusting place.

Cheryl's Story

I was the oldest of four girls in my family. My earliest memory of my father is from sometime in the toddler years (I remember being in a baby bed) and is of him tickling me. Tickling graduated to my sitting on his lap, being touched some more, and then sitting on top of him in bed. After a time, he began to expose himself, and he started presenting himself as a toy as part of our playtime. It wasn't threatening or scary. He was very engaging and nurturing, and it just became one of the ways we played. There was no reason to think it wasn't how all daughters and daddies played.

My sisters and I sat in his lap or fell asleep on his chest, but I never remember any affection from my mother. She never held us or expressed any love. There was no rocking or kissing good night. Nothing. So because of her emotional detachment and my father's nonthreatening physical touching, I didn't resent (at first) the "playtimes" with him. I guess when you're desperately thirsty for love and affection, anything is better than nothing. Later, this conditioning set the stage for other perpetrators because my desire to connect with someone was so strong.

As my body developed, my father's abuse turned into full-blown sexual intercourse. I remember waking up to a hand over my mouth, with him on top of me. It happened at least two or three times a week. It hurt a lot — I was still in elementary school, and my dad was six foot three. I would cry quietly, still with his hand muffling any sounds. After he left, I didn't sleep a lot. I was practically a zombie the next day at school, exhausted and trying to shut out the previous night's encounter.

I remember pornography in the house. It wasn't well hidden. He would draw dialogue balloons above pictures of people having sex, and it always illustrated the girl in the picture saying, "Please, Daddy," or some such thing.

When we visited my grandparents, I slept between them in their bed until I was too big. During those nights, my grandfather would reach around me and touch and fondle me, rubbing his erection against my back while my grandmother slept. I've wondered if my grandfather also abused my dad when he was little. I recall pictures of my dad as a child. He looked more like a girl than a little boy. If he had been abused, it would explain a lot.

About this time, something happened that became a turning point. I was in the third grade. One evening, all of the students were giving a concert for the parents. My mom and dad knew about it, but I walked to school that night by myself. Each class had its own song to sing, and then the whole third grade came back onstage to sing "Amazing Grace."

When the program was over, the kids ran down from the stage and into the arms of their families. I stood there and watched for a while and then walked through the auditorium and on home — alone.

That night, the scales fell from my eyes. For the first time, I could see that my family was not like other families. It was such a powerful event that even today when we sing "Amazing Grace" in church, I'm immediately transported back to when I was that little girl on the stage. Though I may not be able to sing "Amazing Grace" all the way through today, I'm determined that someday, perhaps not until heaven, I will stand and sing it in praise.

When I started dating regularly at about thirteen, I was very sexually active. There really weren't any boundaries. My dad's nocturnal visits continued—the same dark figure, the same stealthy approach, always with my sisters in the same room. The only consolation I had, if you could call it that, was that the day after one of his visits, I always got to do whatever I wanted. He would give me money to go anywhere, do anything. It was more or less a reward for compliance.

But around the time I turned fourteen, I noticed my father's attitude toward me changing. He had become what I would call a jealous lover. He nailed the windows shut in our room and then painted them black. He restricted my coming and going and policed my boyfriends. One afternoon, one of my boyfriends came over. My dad had been drinking and started taunting him. Pretty soon it was an out-and-out brawl. I ran and hid in my closet. A few minutes later, my dad came to me, bloody and angry. He said, "I hope you're happy. Look what your boyfriend did." And then he said, still breathing heavily, "At least he can't say he was the first!"

Our situation had clearly changed. About three weeks later, I ran away with this same boyfriend to Corpus Christi, Texas. Before long, I was caught with drugs by the police and thrown into a secure juvenile facility complete with guard dogs and a barbed wire fence. My parents didn't show up for three months, and when they did, they said they had waited that long in order to teach me a lesson about running away. After I got home, my father's night visits started again, as did the jealous behavior.

I started looking for an opportunity to leave for good. My mother wasn't aloof anymore; she had become violent. I remember having to lock myself in the bathroom until my dad got home after she split my head open *while beating me with a big belt buckle. She resented me, I think, because my sisters — whom I had taken care of for all those years — looked to me instead of her for affection. My aunt and I were condemned for assuming the care-giver role she had abandoned.*

By this time, I was making money at school selling drugs. One day I decided to leave home and never go back. I was able to live on the street for over a year, sleeping at a friend's house one night, in someone's car the next, or in a field when neither was an option. My drug use was soaring quickly. I would start with alcohol in the morning and end early the next morning with cocaine, acid, mescaline, or THC. I desperately wanted to escape.

I ended up marrying a guy whose house I slept at frequently. Things were okay for the first couple of years, though I saw right away how badly his dad treated his mom. He would call her stupid or a whore and throw food at her if it didn't taste right. Then he would tell her to clean it up, and she did.

It shouldn't have been too much of a surprise when my then-husband started treating me the same way. It seemed he had to prove himself to his dad, to put his wife in her place just like the old man did. He started drinking more (also like his dad), and the alcohol escalated the violence. He would back me into corners and call me the same names his dad called his mother. He even shoved my face into a plate.

Well, my dad had trained me never to back down. I was determined I wouldn't become a doormat. So when he choked me with a necklace I was wearing, I threw glasses, dishes, or whatever I could find at him. In our last fight, he backed me into a corner and pounded on my left eye. I went to the hospital with a fractured socket and a bruised pupil. I looked like Rocky after his first fight. They drained the blood and relieved the pressure, but my glasses are a reminder today of what that marriage was like.

A few months later, he came home and told me to find another place to live because he didn't want to be married anymore. Almost a year after that, Brad and I met.

Cheryl's abuse involved many perpetrators — her father, grandfather, classmates at school, and husband at the time — and it lasted for many years.

Some survivors we've worked with have shared about single instances of abuse by a trusted relative or family friend. Some have shared experiences of multiple rapes by a group of drunken friends or visiting cousins. Some have vague memories of repeated, methodic abuse that was a part of humiliating and painful rituals watched by a group of people (including family members). Some report being invited to join in sexual acts with a parent and another partner — a third party in a sick fantasy.

Some survivors are reluctant to share for fear their experience does not "measure up" to a horrific-enough standard. But through our support groups, we have learned that people who experience a single event of abuse can have long-term effects just as devastating as those who have experienced years of repeated abuse.

Wherever you have been and wherever you are now, God can bring healing. There is no need to compare yourself, your experiences, or your actions with anyone else. God will meet you where you are:

"Come to me, all you who are weary and burdened, and I will give you rest. Take my yoke upon you and learn from me, for I am gentle and humble in heart, and you will find rest for your souls. For my yoke is easy, and my burden is light." (Matthew 11:28-30, NKJV)

pause & reflect

Stop for a moment to pray. Thank God for His unique and matchless creation: you! Thank Him for His never-ending, faithful desire to meet you and redeem you where you are. Ask His Spirit to open your heart in new ways to receive His love and acceptance.

it just gets better

At this point, you may be starting to understand a little of your past. Hopefully you're beginning to see that your experience of abuse, no matter the details, is just as valid as others' experiences; that you're part of a community of survivors who experience similar pain and confusion; and that God is with you. Yet you know it's much more complex than that, and one of the signs of that complexity is the fact that there's another person involved: your spouse. Your relationship with your spouse is a lifelong commitment, a lifelong commitment that seems like a lifelong challenge when you can barely make a commitment to get out of bed some days. Although this spouse may be someone who looks at you like you're speaking Greek half the time, he's someone you have to love, respect, and trust. Yet how are you supposed to trust someone who has no idea of what you've been through?

It's hard enough to stand in a church on your wedding day, in the presence of God and people who know you well, and pledge eternal loyalty to another person. To do so carrying the baggage of abuse turns your improbable vows into downright scary propositions.

How have you as a couple dealt with this issue of abuse? Is it a source of constant friction, or the elephant in the room that no one will discuss? Assuming either spouse could have a passive or aggressive personality, there are four basic relational combinations that can determine how couples deal with the issue of sexual abuse. These combinations are shown in the following diagram:

On the chart, circle the quadrant number that best describes you as a couple.

	Quadrant #3 Aggressive Spouse Passive Survivor	**Quadrant #4** Aggressive Spouse Aggressive Survivor
Spouse Aggression	**Quadrant #1** Passive Spouse Passive Survivor	**Quadrant #2** Passive Spouse Aggressive Survivor
	Survivor Aggression	

Quadrant 1 couples don't communicate much. They're both afraid of saying the wrong thing, so they say nothing. They're not purposely

secretive, just unsure of what to say. Expressing feelings openly has always been a problem, and it seems easier to sweep conflict under the rug than to face tense feelings or risk being hurt.

Both the survivor and the spouse avoid conflict, and who can blame them? They're afraid to be dependent on anyone; dependency is a sign of weakness, and vulnerability has been punished in the past. Both frequently turn inward, shutting out the community, support network, and objectivity they desperately need. Abuse may be the elephant in the room, but Quadrant 1 couples can still find a way to make all the furniture fit.

These couples will benefit from the accountability discussion in chapter 6.

Quadrant 2 survivors are always in control. Their primary motivation is self-protection; they want to ensure they never will be victimized again. They are often physically and mentally exhausted from managing everything from the family's minute-by-minute schedule, to the outside world's perception of their spiritual health, to their sex life, to where they sit in a room. Nothing can be left to chance.

Quadrant 2 spouses are also very tired, but for different reasons. They're asked for their opinion and then they're shut down. They're blamed for incidents of which they weren't even aware. Though directed to be the protector and leader of the family, they are usually overruled when attempting to exercise that judgment. They often make things worse when trying to help and have learned it is best to give in and not argue. They avoid enough conflict for both of them.

Chapter 5 is especially applicable to this couple.

Survivors in **Quadrant 3** have so internalized their shame that they believe their desires and needs are not important. They are convinced they are unworthy of respect and consideration. Their guilt is so profound and deep-seated that they feel they must take responsibility for it. Believing they are unable to make competent and appropriate decisions, their sense of who they are is lost to a more dominant mate.

Spouses in Quadrant 3 take up the slack of uncertainty, assuming the license to drive all decisions. Cues are often taken from the survivors' hesitancy, and they may unwittingly continue their wife's self-abasement by not asking for opinions or discounting the ones they have made known. These spouses take the wheel, put the car in gear, and take off, whether the seat belts are securely fastened or not.

Survivors in this quadrant (and their spouses) may see themselves, and some specific suggestions for improved communication, in the following chapter on shame.

Quadrant 4 couples sit on stools in opposite corners, waiting for the bell. Aggressive survivors resent authority, regardless of the source. They may have forestalled continued abuse and manipulation by retaliating with equal intensity. This adversarial stance can occasionally scare away or intimidate the opposition, and for them, backing down (or discretion) is never the better part of valor.

Quadrant 4 spouses often reflect back anger as a defense or in desperation because deferral doesn't work. While their relationship is far from hopeless, a Quadrant 4 couple is a recipe for volatility.

Typically, the greatest casualty in Quadrant 4 couples is the sacrifice of relational intimacy. Chapter 3 focuses on this subject.

now what?

Though God joins every marriage in the same fundamental union, each is a one-of-a-kind concoction. How can we hope to connect? How can we achieve balance? It's hard enough to make a marriage work under normal circumstances with two flawed, unique, and unpredictable people. But add the horrific and humiliating experience of sexual abuse, and the possibilities for a healthy relationship can seem very slim indeed! We might ask, "How can this ever work?"

There is good news: The problem is not yours alone to solve. There is hope in the person of Jesus Christ. He is the only Answer, and with Him in the breach between you — with Him to unite your purposes together and to provide a perfect model — you can and will be drawn together. He can heal you despite your flaws and, yes, even despite the long-term damage of sexual abuse.

This book is designed with one overarching objective: to assist people in becoming more fully devoted followers of Jesus. With this as our objective, hope and healing are sure to come. And as we grow more loving toward God and others, we will foster openness to the regenerative work of the Holy Spirit. The succeeding chapters will help you:

- Recognize your own sin and need for a Savior
- Open yourself to receive healing and understanding from the only true Source, Jesus
- Find hope for the truest and most godlike expression of community this side of heaven: the marriage relationship

As our primary text in Colossians points out, our only true Source of healing is redemption in Christ. The biggest obstacle to Christlikeness is the problem of sin and its influence. As we begin our study of Colossians, the first consequence for us to address is perhaps the most damaging result of the struggle with that sin nature: shame.

overcoming shame

Therefore, as God's chosen people, holy and dearly loved . . .

(Colossians 3:12)

Karen was nine years old when her fourteen-year-old brother approached her. After explaining how much he cared for her and how special she was, he asked a favor. "There are things boys do to show love," he told her. But, he explained, he couldn't do these things with his girlfriend because she was older and might get pregnant. He did, however, want to do those things with Karen because she was a special sister.

Karen did feel special and was grateful for her brother's attention. He moved slowly at first, but soon she willingly allowed her brother to have intercourse with her. She felt honored that he would select her to fulfill his desire. Yet as the years went by, Karen began to understand her brother's deception. Her feeling of being "special" turned to shame that she could have been so gullible and naive.

Her shame deepened further as she recalled the physical pleasure of the sexual acts. *How pitiful must I be,* she thought, *to have enjoyed any part of such a humiliating and sickening act!*

In this chapter, we will look at how shame differs from guilt and how shame can trap us. We'll examine the reproductive nature of shame — how it grows by feeding on itself and multiplying. Most important, we will discuss one of the central themes of the gospel: that Christ not only feels and empathizes with our shame but He also has provided a way out.

shame versus guilt

Shame is not the same as guilt. If a child throws a baseball in the house after being told not to and breaks a vase, he feels guilty for what he did (and probably a little fearful as well). Guilt is regret or remorse concerning an act of the will. Shame is embarrassment of who you *are*.

Survivors such as Karen often feel overwhelming shame because of past events over which they had no control. Survivors will then take on unnecessary guilt as an outgrowth of the shame. They take the blame for almost anything. And for every instance when they "admit" blame, there may be ten others for which they quietly feel it.

They might say, "If I had just opened my eyes or had a little more backbone, the abuse never would have happened." Even when consoled by a friend or spouse, they often still admit blame: "I know children are victimized, but in my case, it really *was* my fault." Survivors put on masks to cover the shame. They become embarrassed by or obsessed with their physical appearance. Shame creates relationship difficulties (discussed at length in the next chapter) and sexual problems (to be discussed in chapter 7). A survivor overwhelmed with shame believes, *It's not just what happened that was bad; it's me. I am bad.*

pause & reflect

Think about these questions and discuss your answers with each other:

1. (Survivor), how is your experience like Karen's? How did your abuser deceive you? How do you feel about having been deceived?

2. (Survivor), if you were talking to Karen today, what words of comfort would you offer?

3. (Spouse), what was your wife's response to question two? Are the words of encouragement she would give to Karen appropriate to reflect back to her?

It's true we are often harder on ourselves than on others. A survivor will generously offer words of healing and comfort to someone else but not believe that those same words can also apply to her. As a spouse, you can reaffirm your wife by reflecting the very same words she might use to encourage someone else.

feeding the monster

Shame is perhaps the most harmful effect of sexual abuse. It is Satan's perfect weapon. Why? Because once shame has begun, it requires little maintenance. That's the nature of shame — it reproduces easily. Like the proverbial "snowball rolling downhill," it grows rapidly and gathers momentum. Before long, it seems impossible to stop.

Let's talk about what feeds this monster, how the cycle begins and is sustained. If we can recognize how it is perpetuated, we can begin to slow its progress. Ideally, we want to stop shame in its tracks, in the same way we'd throw a stick between the spokes of a bicycle wheel to bring it to an abrupt halt.

There are three main ingredients to abuse survivors' shame: humiliation, devaluation, and propagation.

Humiliation. As a survivor, you probably experienced both physical and emotional humiliation. You may have suffered the physical humiliation of having to undress in front of your perpetrator. Perhaps a large part of your abuse was having been ogled. You might have been forced to watch your perpetrator undress, expose himself, or masturbate in front of you.

You might have felt emotional humiliation when you begged him to stop but he didn't; when your perpetrator ignored you afterward, as if the event never happened; or when your pleas to be valued outside of a dark bedroom went unanswered.

One woman we know was forced at twelve years old to have sex with her divorced father every night. Even though she purposely slept on her stomach, he still managed to have intercourse with her most nights. Inevitably, after he was through, he would ask, "Why did you let me do that?" He would then instruct his daughter to "never let me do that again."

Not only was blame skillfully transferred to her, her sense of shame and humiliation grew daily. She condemned herself for being so weak, for being the kind of person that would allow him to do that *again*.

Her self-abasement, like that of most survivors, was both physical and emotional. The message was — and is — loud and clear: Your desires, your zone of privacy, your needs, and your self-regard are meaningless. You exist only to meet someone else's needs. There's no reason to believe that your wants are important.

Devaluation. Humiliation continues until the survivor reaches a new point of vulnerability: devaluation of the truth. This second phase comes after the abuse or later in life and happens when others refuse to believe what you endured.

When abuse is reported to a parent or other authority figure, the charges are often discounted, dismissed, or rationalized. Families ostracize survivors for stirring up trouble, making accusations, and raising issues that disturb the family's sense of equilibrium. Mothers can be especially torn by having to choose between their child's claim of abuse and stability in the marriage. No matter the evidence presented, mothers frequently choose not to believe such a horrific act could happen.

A survivor may also have opened up to a pastor, only to hear her abuse rationalized or excused. This devaluation of truth maintains her humiliation. She's been rejected all over again! Then self-doubt mushrooms, and she finds herself saying, "I trusted an enabler rather than a protector! When will I learn?" Shame is reinforced, and Satan wins another round.

Propagation. Shame, frustration, and disappointment spread as the survivor becomes aware of the isolation, anger, and bitterness abuse can produce in her. She may become fearful that the cycle will repeat and she will once again feel powerless to change her behavior. It's difficult to trust people, regardless of their distance from the abuse events. The need to protect and control continues the survivor's shame and intensifies her feelings of vulnerability.

Here's one more significant characteristic of this circular pattern: It is centrifugal — that is, it is outward-driving, pushing feelings and people away from the survivor. The circle spirals away from the center, increasing her feelings of seclusion and desolation. And it can be *very* difficult to stop. With the removal of community, the Enemy denies the wounded valuable resources.

Picture the nature specials you've seen on TV. A documentary follows a lion, tiger, or other predator as it stalks a herd, selecting a victim to separate from the others. It selects an animal that is weak, crippled, or very young because it can be most easily isolated, is the most unsure, or is the slowest. As the chase begins, the predator segregates the intended victim from the herd and makes an easy kill.

Satan wants to separate survivors from community. By creating a centrifugal atmosphere of shame that pushes other people away, he scatters the resources survivors need most. It is critical to see through and sabotage this tactic, and to do so, survivors must intentionally reach out to others. Moving toward community is one of the most effective tools to combat Satan's plan of division.

some good news

Shame targets the very heart of our self-image and becomes a deeply rooted lie. Have you ever encountered a weed in a garden so stubborn, so deeply and intricately rooted that it doesn't seem to end? This is the nature of shame and its effect on self-esteem. We begin to believe that if our perpetrators didn't value us or care for us, we must not deserve any better. Our loathing then turns inward, and we come full circle to becoming ashamed of not just wht happened but who we are.

But here's the good news: You are not defined by shame. The definition of who you are was settled once and for all on the Cross and cannot be undone, diminished, or spoiled. You can believe who God says you are: a person of infinite value, a person worth the sacrifice of His Son to restore the value you never may have felt before. You have been bought at a price (see 1 Corinthians 6:20). If you have trusted Christ for your salvation and have resolved to live your life for Him, you are:

- Chosen and dearly loved (Colossians 3:12) — our key verse for this chapter
- The light of the world (Matthew 5:14)
- The temple of God (1 Corinthians 3:16)
- God's workmanship (Ephesians 2:10)
- A child of God (John 1:12)
- A member of Christ's body (1 Corinthians 12:27)
- A completely new creation (2 Corinthians 5:17)
- A letter from Christ, written with the Spirit of God (2 Corinthians 3:3)

In Christ, you have a new definition of worth. Your ownership of that shame can cease; you can walk away!

There are two passages in 2 Corinthians that illustrate this hope:

Indeed, in our hearts we felt the sentence of death. But this happened that we might not rely on ourselves but on God, who raises the dead. (1:9)

Not that we are competent in ourselves to claim anything for ourselves, but our competence comes from God. (3:5)

Of course, that sounds easier than it is! Shame keeps us in bondage, chained to the past.

If you've ever been to the circus, you may have noticed a restraint cuff with a chain attached to an elephant's leg. A stake driven into the ground anchors this restraint. Have you ever wondered why an adult elephant, which is more than capable of pulling the stake out of the ground and walking away, chooses to remain chained?

It's because as a baby, the elephant was not strong enough to pull the stake out of the ground. And as the elephant grows, it maintains the "belief" that it can't break the restraint. The handlers are therefore able to control an adult elephant with a device that, in truth, has no power over it.

In the same way, the Enemy deceives you into believing that you are still helpless, unloved, and chained to the past. In Christ, however, we have been set free. God gives us the strength to "pull out the stake" tying us to the past. We no longer need be captive to the shame and cruelty suffered so long ago.

pause &
reflect

1. How does your past shame influence your behavior today?

2. List specific past events in which you realized you felt shame inappropriately. These events may or may not be related to your abuse.

Reflect on what it means to be a child of God (see John 1:12). Offer a prayer of thanksgiving to God for His wonderful gift of grace.

One day a little boy and his sister visited their grandparents' farm. The boy, Johnny, was given a slingshot to play with outside. He practiced in the woods but couldn't hit a single target. Feeling discouraged, he headed back for lunch.

As he was walking back to the farmhouse, he saw his grandma's pet duck. Without thinking, he loaded and released the slingshot, hitting the duck square in the head and killing it. He was shocked and mortified.

In a panic, he hid the dead duck in a woodpile, only to discover his sister watching. Sally had seen it all but said nothing.

After lunch that day, Grandma asked Sally to help with the dishes. Sally said, "Grandma, Johnny told me he wanted to help in the kitchen today, didn't you, Johnny?" And then she whispered to him, "Remember the duck?"

Johnny did the dishes.

Later, Grandpa asked if the children wanted to go fishing. Grandma said, "I'm sorry, but I need Sally to help make supper." Sally smiled and said, "Well, that's all right because Johnny told me he wanted to help." And she whispered again, "Remember the duck?"

Sally went fishing and Johnny stayed behind.

After several days of doing both his chores and Sally's, Johnny finally couldn't stand it any longer. He came to Grandma and confessed that he had killed the duck. She knelt down, gave him a hug, and said, "I know. I was standing at the window and saw the whole thing. But because I love you, I forgave you. I was just wondering how long you would let Sally make a slave of you."

We can unpack two significant truths from this story. The first is that the Enemy wants you to continue in bondage, and as long as you seek esteem from anything other than Christ, you *give* Satan that power to enslave you and keep the wounds open.

The other truth is this: Jesus was standing at the window, and He saw the whole thing. Your abuse grieved Him and hurt Him terribly, just as you would be grieved and hurt by the abuse of your own children. And more than anything else, He wants to embrace you, apply salve to your wounds, and encourage you to take His yoke and find rest for your soul (see Matthew 11:28-30).

the problem of evil

This brings up a dilemma that all survivors, and all believers in Christ, must wrestle with: the presence of evil in the world. If Jesus *was* standing at the window and saw the whole thing, how could He have let this happen? Why didn't He stop it? Doesn't He care?

The fancy two-dollar word for this issue is *theodicy*. Theodicy is the dilemma of affirming God's goodness and providence in a fallen world full of evil. It is coming to grips with a God who creates man as a free moral agent with unlimited choices; a God whose sense of timing and justice don't often square with our own; a God who is actively involved with His people, but who, for reasons often unexplained, permits suffering and pain.

In his wonderful book *Wishful Thinking: A Theological ABC*, Frederick Buechner addresses the existence of evil in the world:

God is all-powerful.

God is all-good.

Terrible things happen.

You can reconcile any two of these propositions with each other, but you can't reconcile all three. The problem of evil is perhaps the biggest single problem for religious faith.

There have been numerous theological and philosophical attempts to solve it, but when it comes down to the reality of evil itself they are none of them worth much. When a child is raped and murdered, the parents are not apt to take much comfort from the explanation (better than most) that since God wants man to love him, man must be free to love or not to love and thus free to rape and murder a child if he takes a notion to.

Christian Science solves the problem of evil by saying that it does not exist except as an illusion of mortal mind. Buddhism solves it in terms of reincarnation and an inexorable law of cause and effect whereby the raped child is merely reaping the consequences of evil deeds it committed in another life.

Christianity, on the other hand, ultimately offers no theoretical solution at all. It merely points to the cross and says that, practically speaking, there is no evil so dark and so obscene — not even this — but that God can turn it to good.[3]

Ultimately, we must choose to believe that God does in fact love us and desire the best for us. Despite our doubt, we can *choose* to continue to seek God. He created the world, but He did not introduce evil into it. On the contrary, He introduced a pathway to reconciliation and healing. In the face of so much betrayal, God alone is completely trustworthy and promises to "repay you for the years the locusts have eaten" (Joel 2:25).

a big step

It *is* possible to recover from the weight of the shame you've carried. In our support groups, one thing has had the most profound effect on a survivor's path to freedom: telling her story. It must be done with care, but releasing what has held you for so long can be a dramatic step in walking away from shame. It has the effect of dilution — disclosing what happened to you in a safe, trusting environment means you don't carry that burden alone. We've found that when the "unshackling" takes place among others who understand and can affirm your experience, it produces a powerful freedom.

Telling your story also reduces the toxic effect of the secrecy (as it did for Johnny). It can help you, perhaps for the first time, label what happened as "wrong." It was *not* your fault.

A few suggestions as you consider this:

Be choosy. You have the power now, not your perpetrator. You can choose your audience. At some point, we hope you can share with your spouse, but you might want to start with a trusted friend or support group.

Disclose at your own pace. You may not be able to put everything on the table at once, and that's okay. You are in charge of what you reveal and when.

Share what you remember. Don't be intimidated by an incomplete memory. God has promised we won't be given more than we can handle (see 1 Corinthians 10:13). By His grace, you might remember more as you're able to cope with it; if you don't, it's not reason for self-doubt.

Write about what happened. Your letter or journal need not be addressed to anyone in particular. What you write can give you something to disclose later when you approach a trusted friend or relative.

When you're ready to share, be specific. Your self-acquittal will be most complete when you are able to share exactly what you remember.

shame was conquered

In the story of Johnny and his sister, Johnny eventually admitted his act and came to terms with an unmerited offer of grace. That offer is available to all of us through the Cross. The Cross demonstrates that there is no past so dark or shadowed — not even yours — that God cannot use it for good. After His death, Jesus was not ashamed of His wounds. He showed them to Thomas as marks of His ordeal and death. Because of the Cross, Jesus understands your suffering.

This chapter closes with a story of redemption and renewed worth.

A water bearer in India had two large pots, hung on each end of a pole, which he carried across his neck. One of the pots had a crack in it; the other was whole and intact. The undamaged pot always delivered a full portion of water at the end of the long walk from the stream to the master's house; the cracked pot always arrived only half full.

For a full two years this went on daily, with the bearer delivering only one and a half pots of water to his master's house each day. The cracked pot was ashamed of its own imperfection and miserable because it was able to accomplish only half of what it had been made to do.

After two years of what it perceived to be bitter failure, it spoke to the water bearer one day by the stream.

"I am ashamed of myself, and I want to apologize to you."

"Why?" asked the bearer. "What are you ashamed of?"

"For these past two years, I have been able to deliver only half my load because this crack in my side causes water to leak out all the way back to your master's house. Because of my flaws, you have to do all of this work, and you don't get full value from your efforts," the pot said.

The water bearer felt sorry for the old cracked pot, and in his compassion, he said, "As we return to the master's house, I want you to notice the beautiful flowers along the path."

Indeed, as they went up the hill, the old cracked pot took notice of the sun warming the beautiful wildflowers on the side of the path, and this cheered it some. But at the end of the trail, it still felt bad because it had leaked out half its load, and so again it apologized to the bearer for its failure.

The bearer said to the pot, "Did you notice that there were flowers on your side of the path but not on the other side? That's because I have always known about your flaw, and I have used it for my master's glory. I planted flower seeds on your side of the path, and every day when we walk back from the stream, you've watered them. For two years I have been able to pick these *beautiful flowers to decorate my master's table. If you were not just the way you are, he would not have this beauty to grace his house."*

Like the cracked pot, have you heard these tapes playing in the back of your mind?

- "I'm damaged goods."
- "I've been messed up for so long that no one would care for me or have a use for me."
- "I might as well give up on myself — God surely has."

Satan wants to keep those tapes playing in an endless loop, to keep you oppressed and in bondage. But Jesus offers a cutting torch to begin to dismantle the chains that have shackled you. Listen to the message God offers to counteract those negative tapes:

"So do not fear, for I am with you;
do not be dismayed, for I am your God.
I will strengthen you and help you;
I will uphold you with my righteous right hand.
All who rage against you
will surely be ashamed and disgraced;
those who oppose you
will be as nothing and perish.
Though you search for your enemies,
you will not find them.

Those who wage war against you

> will be as nothing at all.

For I am the LORD, your God,

> who takes hold of your right hand

and says to you, Do not fear;

> I will help you." (Isaiah 41:10-13)

pause & reflect

1. What is your reaction to the truth that you were "bought at a price"? How does it feel to be indebted for such a gift?

2. How does the magnitude of God's gift make you feel?

3. What specific action steps can you take, as a couple, to reaffirm each other's worth in Christ?

We have seen the impact of shame and the remedy Christ offers to all who will accept His gift. Next, we will explore how shame can affect relational intimacy.

restoring
relational intimacy

Clothe yourselves with compassion, kindness, humility, gentleness and patience. Bear with each other and forgive whatever grievances you may have against one another. Forgive as the Lord forgave you. (Colossians 3:12-13)

I f you throw a rock straight up in the air, it will go up for a while, but quickly the upward motion will slow and stop. The rock will then fall back to earth because of gravity. However, if you could throw a rock at a speed of twenty-five thousand miles per hour, it would continue into space, having met the minimum "escape velocity" — the speed required for an object to escape the earth's gravitational pull.

Now imagine a mass in space so dense and with such a gravitational force that not even light traveling at 186,000 miles per *second* can escape. Scientists believe there is such a mass — it's called a black hole. Although black holes can't be observed directly because no light can escape their gravitational pull, scientists don't doubt their existence. Why? Because they observe *what happens around the black holes*. By applying the laws of physics, they deduce their existence.

In a similar way, we can deduce what is going on in the lives of individuals by examining what's happening around them.

where we're going

In this chapter, we will deal with the fallout of our abuse and shame, particularly their effect on our capacity to build loving relationships with our spouses, our families, and the world.

Read again the key verse for this chapter:

Clothe yourselves with compassion, kindness, humility, gentle-ness and patience. Bear with each other and forgive whatever grievances you may have against one another. Forgive as the Lord forgave you. (Colossians 3:12-13)

Have you ever noticed how difficult it is to make correct assumptions about people until they interact with others? Observing people in a vacuum tells you only what they want you to see. You may draw conclusions about them based on their physical appearance, but until you see them in a community setting, who they really are remains a mystery.

In this respect, people and black holes have a lot in common. You can learn a lot about people based on what happens around them. What goes on around a person is also a good barometer of the work of the Spirit. Jesus stated this clearly in the Sermon on the Mount when He said, "By their fruit you will recognize them" (Matthew 7:16).

healing and victimhood

Many survivors of sexual abuse had to develop defense mechanisms to equip themselves to live in a damaging community or environment — and many of those defense mechanisms are carried into their later behavior. Survivors affect people around them by the way they adapt to their surroundings, whether they put on disguises like chameleons or retreat into their shells like turtles. When survivors flee or retreat, they're often unable to give or receive affection, express feelings constructively, or release even the smallest of debts.

Everything around survivors is absorbed and swept into the vortex of their feelings — a "black hole of emotion." Trust doesn't come easily, making relational intimacy (with a husband, family, or friends) very difficult. When healthy people make overtures to wounded people, they may fall into a bottomless pit from which nearly nothing (including reciprocal kindness, vulnerability, or trust) can extract them.

For several years, Cathy was unable to refer to herself as a "survivor." When talking about her past abuse, she was always a "victim." She harbored many grudges — some due to her abuse, others due to perceived insults or innocent misunderstandings. Cathy's self-image was so poor that people around her spent most of their time proving to her again and again that they cared. She required her family and friends to jump through these hoops because it was the only thing she accepted as proof of their steadfast affection.

As a result, Cathy's ability to establish intimacy with her husband, family, fellow church members, and even God was always compromised. This "victimhood" had, in a way, become a black hole of emotion from which nothing could be released.

Cathy's husband was caught in this whirlpool with her. He could never do enough to satisfy her needs and tired quickly of trying. Can you identify with Cathy or her husband? As a survivor, have you ever been too demanding of others with your expectations? As a spouse, have you ever been tempted to give up?

This self-isolation and repelling of others can take many forms. Here are some typical signs:

- Refusing to give the benefit of the doubt
- Assuming the worst motives of others
- A persistent need to correct everyone
- Holding others at arm's length
- Insistence on repeated apologies for past actions
- Inability to forgive and release grudges

What is the common thread throughout all of these behaviors? You guessed it: an unhealthy focus on oneself.

pause & reflect

1. List some things that are caught in your "gravitational pull."

2. What are the areas of hypersensitivity in your life? How do these manifest themselves in your relationships?

3. What steps can you take together to combat the victimhood syndrome and release others from this never-ending burden of proof?

emotional withdrawal

When the body experiences great trauma, its natural response is to protect itself and direct energy to its most critical functions. Sometimes after a severe accident, a person's body will go into a coma, conserving energy and stopping unnecessary functions in order to focus on rest and self-healing. When we are confronted with danger, a variety of chemical changes occurs that increases our awareness, tenses our muscles, and biologically prepares us to face the threat. We are automatically redirected to an inward focus that will sustain us through the danger.

To survive the emotional trauma of abuse, many survivors curl into a similarly protective shell. They turn away emotionally, take a defensive posture to the world, and retreat from others. Why? For self-preservation. By withdrawing and "stiff-arming" those around them, they try to ensure that no one will come close enough again to hurt them. They can't take that risk.

Retreat can be a survivor's preferred response. But there's a problem: We were made for community. We were designed by a Being of community who expressed this fellowship when He said:

> "Let us make man in our image, in our likeness." (Genesis 1:26)

In fact, the very name of God, *Elohim*, is plural. He has always existed in perfect community — in the persons of the Father, Son, and Spirit. And because we were made in God's image, we were designed for community. We see this again just a few verses later when God observed,

> "It is not good for the man to be alone. I will make a helper suitable for him." (Genesis 2:18)

Adam needed someone to complement him, someone to join him in fulfilling God's tasks for humanity. The Enemy would have us deny our need for community, convincing us it's for our own protection and welfare to go without it. If he can get us to refuse the nourishment and wholeness others bring, to walk away from the very thing we were made for, he has won a huge victory.

isolation and self-absorption

It might seem the most unnatural thing in the world to reach for fraternity and fellowship after suffering damage inflicted by others. Yet when we sequester ourselves physically and emotionally, we lose the blessing and comfort of community. We see the world through only one set of lenses — our own. We begin to behave in ways that serve only our community of one.

During a Sunday sermon, a preacher explained (with tongue in cheek) to his congregation that he was convinced the only physical change to a person's body after death was that the elbows locked. He imagined all people, whether in torment or in paradise, existed in this state, unable to bend their arms. His vision of hell was of frustrated souls who were eternally starving, unable to feed themselves because of their locked elbows. His vision of heaven was of eternally happy and satisfied saints who were never hungry because they took great pleasure in feeding each other.

C. S. Lewis alluded to the same issue in his book *The Great Divorce*.[4] He spoke of a bus that transported people from hell to heaven. When the bus arrived from the gray damp fog of hell to the bright color and clarity of heaven, the hellish people felt the grass of heaven as spikes in their feet. Lewis's point was that they had brought hell with them to heaven. In their self-absorption, they became unable to experience beauty and joy. Their capacity to participate in the lives of others was directly proportional to their capacity to let go of themselves. At the end of the story, all but one of the travelers chose to return to hell.

They *chose* to go back because they could not escape themselves and only in hell would they be able to keep their self-absorption and victimhood intact.

This principle is at the heart of Paul's teaching on relational harmony and intimacy. Detachment, even if it's caused by the sin and insensitivity of others, is damaging to our lives and our relationships.

pause &
reflect

1. Self-protection was necessary when you were in the midst of abuse. How can you widen your circle of community to allow your spouse to minister to you?

2. If perfect trust were possible, who would you most want around you to support you?

3. As it was for characters in *The Great Divorce*, are there some godly, pure things that have become painful for you? Share them with your spouse.

secrecy

Keeping secrets is another way survivors preserve self-focus in a relationship, and it is one of the biggest obstacles to relational intimacy.

In the last chapter, we talked about the importance of opening up to trusted friends. Secrets sometimes seem necessary for survival, but they can produce overwhelming distance between spouses. You might believe you can't tell your spouse some things. You might even be able to justify this withholding. Perhaps you've thought or spoken the following:

• "What happened to me was too humiliating to bring up."

- "What I did later as a result of my abuse was awful, and I'm too ashamed to talk about it."
- "My spouse would think so much less of me if he knew everything."

Secrecy becomes a cloak of protection. Have you ever wished your spouse would simply accept your choice not to say much about the abuse? Do you consider your spouse insensitive when he asks about your past? Many survivors say, "If you really loved me, you wouldn't ask me to talk about it."

Remember Cathy from earlier in the chapter? When her husband asked why she couldn't fully reveal her past to him, she said it was too painful. While it's very difficult to recount a hurtful past, with Cathy, keeping it to herself was a way to continue her victimhood and retain power over her husband. Every aspect of their relationship was affected, and lack of relational intimacy was to blame.

forgiveness

Relational intimacy can never be achieved without an extension of grace. By contrast, forgiveness can be one of the most difficult things for a survivor to process. Often those who haven't suffered abuse don't understand why this is such a problem. With equal measures of sincerity and bewilderment, they ask, "Why can't you just forgive and forget?"

Chances are, as a survivor, you've heard this more than once. Embracing forgiveness is one of a survivor's most difficult challenges. This is true for several reasons:

- Survivors often feel that forgiveness would minimize the evil of the acts and let the perpetrators off the hook.

- Survivors sometimes believe they can maintain control over the perpetrators by continuing to hold their actions over them. (One of Satan's many lies is that resentment hurts the one resented instead of the one doing the resenting.)

- Survivors may take some responsibility for the abuse, so forgiveness of the perpetrators is nearly impossible because they haven't yet forgiven themselves.

- Survivors usually feel resentment, which breeds anger, and anger blinds them to grace.

- This malice keeps the wound fresh and focuses attention on the injury instead of the recovery.

The key to breaking this cycle is found in the last part of this chapter's key Scripture passage: "Forgive as the Lord forgave you." Forgiving others can happen only when we understand and accept our own pardon through the Cross.

In Matthew 18:23-35, Jesus tells a sobering story that is for all of us. A king called before him a servant who owed him a debt not even winning the state lottery could pay off. After the servant begged for mercy, the king erased the man's debt.

The same servant then found a friend who had borrowed, in comparison, a small fraction of what the servant had owed. When his friend asked him to extend the same mercy, the wicked servant had him imprisoned. The king was incredulous that this servant was so incapable of passing on the mercy he had been given. In anger, the king had the servant turned over to the jailers to be tortured until his own debt was paid. Presumably, he was never seen nor heard from again.

Refusal of mercy is the central issue of this story. Some might say that this is not a valid comparison to a survivor's situation because the victimization of a child is more heinous than owing someone a few dollars. But we need to remember the key to Jesus' illustration is the lack of appreciation for *our own* forgiveness, forgiveness that is extended hour after hour, day after day, made possible only by the sacrifice of God's Son. To "forgive as the Lord forgave you" — as *you* have been reprieved — is critical in cultivating relational intimacy.

A few last words about forgiveness: It is not absolution. It is not forgetting. It does not lessen the severity of the offense. It does not pretend that the abuse never occurred or didn't have devastating effects.

Forgiveness is the intentional decision *not* to collect a debt. It is saying, "I could continue to resent you, hold your crime over your head, or keep throwing it back in your face. But even though I may not be able to forget, I release you from this liability. Your obligation to atone for your crime has ended. And while I can't promise the injury will never come up again, I *can* say that it won't have the same power over me."

pause & reflect

Recall one specific incident from your past that you need to communicate to your spouse (it may or may not be related to your abuse). Try and share:

- Who was there
- What happened
- The role you played
- How you feel about your participation or role
- What you can do about it now

How can you take a tangible step toward forgiveness? Consider these steps:

- Ask God to shape your heart toward forgiveness.
- Write a letter to the perpetrator (even if you don't mail it).
- Request help or accountability from your spouse in taking the next step.
- Move to resolve a hard-to-unload grudge that has nothing to do with your abuse.

The abuse you suffered caused you to build walls that have been fortified and strengthened over the years. It may seem you've fallen into an inescapable relational black hole, but you haven't. You were *made* for community, and it's possible, with God's help, to live in community among similarly imperfect but loving people.

As you bring back relational intimacy, you'll be ready to take the next step: discovering what it means to be complete through love.

becoming complete through love

And over all these virtues put on love, which binds them all together in perfect unity. (Colossians 3:14)

When our daughters were younger, they ate off of divided plates — those molded plates that have three or four separate compartments — so that the potatoes wouldn't touch the carrots, which couldn't touch the meatloaf, which absolutely *could not* touch the rolls. Our daughters' fear was that the different foods would somehow make contact. When we tried to explain that it all wound up in the same place anyway, they were incredulous. I think they truly believed their stomachs had similar compartments!

Despite our telling them that the different foods were chosen precisely *because* they taste good together, they insisted the meal remain segmented. Have you noticed many couples lead their lives in much the same way?

This chapter continues the theme of relational intimacy by focusing on the key to making it all work: authenticity through love.

Remember Colossians 3:13 from the last chapter? Paul designed a nearly complete wardrobe for us to wear: compassion, kindness, humility, gentleness, patience, forbearance, and forgiveness. In this chapter, we complete the ensemble by putting on love. We increase our relational intimacy by *not* compartmentalizing the interaction between us.

It's easy to live our lives with no heartfelt commitment, with perhaps only an occasional bump into each other to remind ourselves we're still married. We fall into a habit of supporting one another from arm's length. All the right things are done and said in an emotional vacuum, earning "brownie points" and avoiding conflict.

God challenges us to go beyond simply doing and saying the right things. Going through the motions (performing kind or compassionate acts) while omitting the unifying principle of love feeds compartmentalization. God tells us that love must hold all of our efforts together.

We'll spend time in this chapter looking at key barriers to intimacy and completeness — ways we keep ourselves emotionally compartmentalized — and discovering how to come together again.

seeing things holistically

Our key verse says that love binds all these admirable qualities "together in perfect unity." Paul used the same phrase in Colossians 2:19, where he warns us not to "[lose] connection with the Head [Christ], from whom the whole body, supported and held together by its ligaments and sinews, grows as God causes it to grow." There is a companion passage in Ephesians:

> Instead, speaking the truth in love, we will in all things grow up into him who is the Head, that is, Christ. From him the whole body, joined and held together by every supporting ligament, grows and builds itself up in love, as each part does its work. (Ephesians 4:15-16)

Without ligaments, our bodies would be unconnected, limp piles of bones, like unanimated puppets without strings. Ligaments are bands of fibrous tissue that connect bones and cartilage, form joints, and hold organs in place. They are the glue of the skeletal system, and they have three main purposes: unifying, holding together, and stabilizing.

Just as ligaments allow the human body's individual bones to move in concert and in one direction, love *unifies* our actions toward each other with one common purpose: loving others as ourselves (see Mark 12:31).

In the same way, ligaments also *hold together*, or cement, our bones. Without this connecting mechanism, individual bones and muscles are of little value. Similarly, without the adhesive of love, the virtues of compassion, kindness, and forgiveness have no coordinated purpose. They have no meaning and depth, and their functions would be hollow and stilted, just like the movement of unconnected muscle.

And finally, just as ligaments *stabilize* the relative position of skeleton and organs so that everything remains connected and in place, love stabilizes a marriage through difficult times, keeping us connected and giving assurance of a mutual commitment.

Love is the catalyst that stimulates and gives meaning to the mercy shown us by God, as well as the mercy we are called to offer in the communion of husband and wife and as brother and sister.

pause & reflect

1. Identify any areas in your relationship in which your words and actions do not match.

2. How can you involve your heart more in your attempts to do the right thing in your marriage relationship?

3. What steps can you take to become more authentic with each
   other?

applying the metaphor

How does this ligament metaphor apply to a marriage affected by sexual abuse? Attempts at kindness or understanding in the absence of true sincerity are largely meaningless, just as unconnected bone and muscles are useless to your body. It may seem on the surface that "doing nice things" should be enough to placate a needy spouse, especially if you are unclear about the nature or depth of the problem in the first place. It's not. As the spouse of a survivor, that can be truly frustrating. You may wonder why you must suffer for the sins and perversions of others, but remember that your spouse has been asking this same question for a long time. She has repeatedly questioned the fairness of paying such a costly emotional and physical price for another's dysfunction.

It's hard to resist trying to answer questions that are, in the end, often unanswerable. We are called to listen carefully and love well. Jesus Himself shows us how to do so in one of the most moving encounters in all of Scripture: the death of Lazarus.

In the eleventh chapter of John's gospel, Jesus receives word that His friend Lazarus is very ill. At the time He receives this news, Jesus is already aware of several things:

- Lazarus will die.
- He will raise him from the dead to demonstrate God's power so the disciples will believe He is who He says He is.
- Prior to the miracle, He will be met with difficult and emotionally wrenching questions as to the necessity of Lazarus's death in light of Jesus' power and, by implication, the length of time it took Him to arrive after receiving word of the sickness.

Despite this awareness, Jesus waits two additional days before setting off for Judea. When He gets there and is met with the conflicted and troubled statement "Lord, if you had been here, my brother would not have died" (John 11:21), He does not do what any of us would be inclined to do. He does not tease them by alluding to a coming miracle they clearly do not expect. He does not offer shopworn adages such as "Time heals all wounds" or even explain to the family how it is "God's will." He does not minimize or invalidate their suffering by telling them to get over it. He doesn't scold them because they blamed Him (of all people) for the death itself. He does not chastise them for their lack of faith in His ability to change the course of nature.

Before the miracle — and in spite of the caustic, careless remarks of both Mary and Martha — He is consumed by His abiding, selfless love for the pain of His friends, and He merely stops and weeps with them.

As spouses of survivors, we are called to do the same. It's just that simple — and just that difficult. How many times do we instead outline a process or diagram a fix? Love goes beyond process, surrounding with grace even poorly implemented attempts to reach out with care and concern.

pause & reflect

1. (Spouse), what are one or two specific things you can do to minister to your wife in a simple, supportive way?

Reflect on the unfair treatment suffered by Jesus. Spend a few moments in worship, praising Him for the love that drove Him to suffer unjustly for you.

completeness

The last phrase of our key passage is translated in the NIV as "perfect unity." Other versions translate the phrase as "the perfect bond of unity" or "together in perfection." The literal Greek is translated as "the bond of completeness." Selfless love in its truest form brings wholeness and maturity to a relationship and provides everything, or *completes* what both parties need. Why? Precisely because it *is* selfless. Selfless love asks nothing of its receiver but gives everything.

This is one of the most important keys to building (or rebuilding) a close relationship. But there are barriers threatening to block our ability to be complete. They pull our focus away from accepting another's offer of selfless love. Here are just a few of these barriers.

Codependency. When a person's self-worth is entirely contingent on the approval of another, we call that person codependent. Codependent behavior can't build healthy boundaries and care for self, often to the detriment of both parties. In contrast to a relationship that seeks completeness, codependent relationships seek mutually compatible *incompleteness.* This is a flawed picture of what the Bible teaches about dependency. Biblically based dependency comes from vulnerability — a confession and surrender of our weaknesses — and not from a mindset that says, "You provide my missing pieces."

Withholding. Remember your first paycheck from your first job? It was likely a sobering event. You probably wondered, *Who is FICA, and why is he taking so much of my money?* Welcome to the world of withholding.

A similar kind of withholding can block completeness in relationships. Spouses or survivors who withhold important feelings essentially give a vote of no confidence to the other party. Because they can't be sure of a compassionate response to their feelings, they choose not to share them at all. This gives the spouse an incomplete picture of what's going on and, by default, builds relational walls between them.

Isolation. For a variety of reasons, survivors and spouses sometimes exclude each other from the most meaningful and satisfying parts of their lives. They take separate vacations. They develop distinctly different friendship circles. They participate in recreational activities apart from each other. One spouse we know spent thirty thousand dollars on an expensive sailboat and moored it at a lake two hours from his home. He enjoyed his prime recreational activity far from the reach of his wife and young children, even though he insisted that the boat was *for* the family. Two years after the purchase, his wife still had no idea where the boat was docked or how to find it. Isolation, when taken to an extreme, dismantles relationships.

Revenge. Spouses can become so frustrated and confused by behavior they don't understand that they withhold their feelings simply out of vengeance. Because they believe their wives should be able to manage these issues, spouses often reciprocate with a "taste of their own medicine."

Sexual dysfunction. A potential problem area for all marriages, sexuality is particularly tenuous in marriages marred by abuse, given the perversion of the sexual act experienced at an early age. Unhealthy sexual behavior by either the survivor or spouse — such as gravitation toward pornography, excessive masturbation, and extramarital affairs — has a drastic impact on a couple's intimacy. This subject is explored further in chapter 7.

pause & **reflect**   Take a moment to pray together for God to bless your sexual relationship. If you've never done this before, don't be discouraged or embarrassed; remember, He invented sex! His plan from the beginning has been a unique oneness between husband and wife.

the role of trust

There is one more barrier to finding unity as a couple, and it is one of the most puzzling dynamics in a relationship between survivors and spouses: the issue of trust.

I knew of Cheryl's sexual abuse from very early in our relationship. I never could understand how she could have made such a poor choice in a first husband, having just fled an abusive environment at home. "Couldn't you see this coming?" I used to ask. "How could you have possibly been attracted to someone who was obviously just as untrustworthy? And why in the world didn't you just leave when he began to beat you up?"

I failed to grasp one of the key dynamics in many survivors' relationships. After repeated betrayals by her perpetrators (her father and grandfather) and the enabler (her mother), Cheryl was drawn to a relationship with someone who was *known* to be untrustworthy. I couldn't understand it, but she was drawn to him precisely *because* he was untrustworthy. Because she knew he was unreliable, there was little risk or danger of being disappointed or betrayed.

For some survivors, committing to a healthy relationship poses the greatest risk of all, for in that relationship lies the possibility of *unexpected* betrayal and disappointment. This fear of betrayal breeds distrust that can linger even if the survivor enters into a loving, nurturing, and positive relationship. That lingering distrust can become a barrier to completeness in the relationship.

it's worth the risk

The key verse for this chapter speaks of a love that is selfless and mature — a love that is both confident and trusting. Loveless actions produce empty relationships. Remember the Pharisees? They had the law on their side, had all the right ingredients in their recipe. But when it came to blending it with a submissive heart and adding the leaven of grateful love rather than legalism, they lost sight of the point, and their confection, as it were, fell flat.

Paul said completeness rooted in selfless love requires us to accept risk. Is there the possibility for rejection? Certainly — and we need look no further than the Cross to see what the worst effects of that rejection can be.

The love shown the world by God's sacrifice of His own Son is the supreme example of selfless love that has the ability to bind all of us together. God knew the risks; He even knew the outcome. But out of inconceivable love, He allowed His perfect community to be broken as Jesus took on the sins of the world. To Him, it was worth the risk to bring us back.

Will you step out and allow your spouse to try, in his own imperfect way, to complete you?

pause &
reflect   1. In what ways has codependency taken over Paul's model of selfless love in your relationship? What would you need to do to change your relationship from being codependent to God-dependent?

2. How have you minimized risk in your relationship? How has this impacted communication in your marriage?

3. What steps will you take to entrust more of yourself to your spouse? (If there are things you want to share now, please do so.)

It's a huge challenge to trust and seek completion in our spouses. God has promised He will equip us if we step out in faith.

The journey toward restoration continues, but we still have a ways to go. There is perhaps no larger speed bump on the road to mutual dependence and surrender than the need for control. The next chapter helps us learn how to relinquish it.

relinquishing control

Let the peace of Christ rule in your hearts, since as members of one body you were called to peace. And be thankful.

(Colossians 3:15)

"The exploratory-assertive motivational system? What's that?" I asked as we headed for the fourteenth tee.

In response, Joe told me the story of the blind baby who smiled.

A psychiatrist was working with an infant who had been born blind. At eight weeks, the baby had not yet smiled, something infants with eyesight do at roughly four weeks. This was no huge surprise. How could a blind infant be expected to smile? He could not see his own mother's smiling face.

Doctors experimented with different sounds in an effort to stimulate the baby. They introduced small bells into the area around his cradle. The sound of the bells did not make the baby smile — at least, not in the beginning.

Then the doctors rigged an apparatus that allowed the infant to control the sound of the bells by kicking his legs. The baby quickly got the hang of it. He kicked. He heard a bell ring. He kicked again. The bell rang again.

Finally the baby smiled. He smiled every time his kicking produced the bell sound, even though the sound of the bells had never caused him to smile before.

What pleased the infant was not the sound of the bell, per se — it was *causing* the sound of the bell. He smiled because he discovered he could make something happen around him. He could manipulate his environment.

Making something happen in the environment around us gives us a sense of competence, which in turn gives us pleasure. A baby will indefatigably use his arms and legs to push the pieces of a mobile hanging above his crib simply for the pleasure of seeing them move in response to his actions. A golfer will happily spend hours on the practice range hitting little white balls to a flag 150 yards away. Both the baby and the golfer are impelled by the same instinct.

where we're going

This chapter deals with the most common behavior resulting from sexual abuse: the need for control. We will consider various forms this need for control can take, look at a scene from the Gospels where Jesus faced the temptation to exert control, and discuss ways to battle the most frequent by-product of control issues: anger.

It's not surprising that survivors have a need for control. While being victimized, they were powerless to set their own boundaries or make their own choices. They were overpowered and unable to withdraw from a situation that was confusing and uncomfortable. They were, both literally and figuratively, pinned down without escape.

For some survivors, this feeling of helplessness intensified after the abuse event because they were too ashamed to tell anyone or because no one believed them if they did. As a result, many have vowed never to be vulnerable again. They promise never again to feel defenseless, and they remain constantly on guard to prevent the possibility of those situations reoccurring. They say, "I have to be in control of my life to ensure I will never be hurt, shamed, or used again."

how control manifests itself

In our key verse for this chapter, Paul wrote, "Let the peace of Christ rule in your hearts." The need for control essentially eliminates a sense of peace for survivors. This happens in a number of ways, including the following.

Resistance to spontaneity. When her husband would make suggestions such as "Let's have the Smiths over tomorrow" or "Let's get away this weekend" or even "Want to fool around?" Jessica always resisted and sometimes became hostile. Spontaneity and last-minute changes threatened her need for control and disrupted a carefully planned schedule. It didn't matter if that schedule was filled with relatively unimportant tasks: She couldn't handle the surprise of something unexpected, and she didn't enjoy feeling as if she were out of the loop in the decision-making process.

Planning for escape. Whenever she took a seat in a room, Rachel insisted on sitting close to a door or at least facing a door. She needed to know that there was always a way out nearby. In a large room, such as an auditorium or church sanctuary, she would sit at the end of a row or in the very back. That way, if anything was said or done that made her uncomfortable, she could simply leave. By providing a means for escape, she maintained a semblance of control over otherwise unpredictable circumstances.

Inflexibility. Vicki required (of both her husband and her children) uncompromising, dutiful adherence to her way of doing things. She would say things such as "That is *not* the way you load the dishwasher" or "Didn't I tell you to vacuum upstairs first?" If family members didn't follow her specific instructions, they would receive a lecture on the consequences of noncompliance. Vicki controlled her family's actions — even well-meaning actions — by saying, "Do this the way I want it done or it's wrong."

Manipulation. Marie maintained her sense of control by manipulating her husband. She would make statements such as "I can tell you don't really care about me or my feelings, because if you did, you would have asked what I thought before [doing this or that]." Inducing guilt, finding fault, and leveraging people against each other helped her believe she could manage her environment.

Busyness. Carol was a workaholic — not because she had a job outside the home but because she felt she could never do enough. This feeling stemmed from her inability to make her father stop touching and fondling her. She often asked herself, *What will it take for me to be effective? To see results?* Her constant motion and busyness was an endless pursuit to control her life in a way she could not when she was a child.

Maintaining a perfect image. Jamie spent a lot of energy carefully maintaining her friends' perception of her as wife and mother. She even became defensive when she felt that perception slip. It was important for her to feel she controlled what others thought about her. (We will discuss this more in the next chapter.)

Can you see now why survivors have a hard time feeling at peace? Those are only a few of the manifestations of control in a survivor's life. Which have you seen or experienced in your own life?

pause & reflect
with your spouse.

1. Describe to your spouse how an episode of your abuse robbed you of control. Share this

2. What does the need for control look like in your life?

the greatest lie and the hardest truth

Chapter 2 dealt at length with shame and its origin: Satan's deceptions and his misrepresentation of who is responsible for the abuse. He uses the same kind of delusion to fool survivors into believing the Greatest Lie of survivorship: "The quest for control works. You can manipulate your environment to minimize risk." What Satan doesn't want you to see is the truth behind that lie — the Hardest Truth. Put simply, the Hardest Truth is: "Your quest for control actually produces bondage and slavery to that which you seek to control."

Whatever we try to control actually controls us. The Enemy's sleight of hand manufactures the belief that not only is it possible to achieve control but, once we do, we're finally set free from powerlessness and helplessness. He cons us into believing:

- We can be the masters of our own fate.
- We will never again be subject to people or circumstances.
- We can coerce submission to get our way.
- We are free.

In reality, we are in chains. We've become what Paul, in Romans 8:15, called "a slave again to fear." Why do we become duped like this? The main reason is that the desire for control appears to be a most logical response to a heart that has been wounded and betrayed. It makes perfect sense to take precautionary measures against the possibility of revictimization. Why leave yourself open? Why be careless?

Unfortunately, the belief that our control will fix things is 180 degrees from Jesus' teachings. It is completely antithetical to everything He taught, preached, and died for. Notice the dialogue and subsequent confrontation between Jesus and Peter in Matthew 16:

> From that time on Jesus began to explain to his disciples that he must go to Jerusalem and suffer many things at the hands of the elders, chief priests and teachers of the law, and that he must be killed and on the third day be raised to life.
>
> Peter took him aside and began to rebuke him. "Never, Lord!" he said. "This shall never happen to you!"
>
> Jesus turned and said to Peter, "Get behind me, Satan! You are a stumbling block to me; you do not have in mind the things of God, but the things of men."

> Then Jesus said to his disciples, "If anyone would come
> after me, he must deny himself and take up his cross and follow
> me. For whoever wants to save his life will lose it, but whoever
> loses his life for me will find it." (21-25)

What a powerful and convicting scene. Reading this story when I was younger, I wondered why Jesus was so hard on Peter. I thought Peter was only trying to protect Jesus and just didn't understand the kind of kingdom He had come to establish. Peter could not imagine this Messiah, the Chosen One of Israel, consigned to such "defeat." There had to be a different ending!

Jesus, however, saw through the temptation and rebuked Satan, the author of this deception. Jesus could see where this line of reasoning was going: "Stay in control here. You won't be any good surrendered to the authorities."

In the same way, the father of lies tries to deceive us. When we compare Satan's lies to Christ's teachings, the truth becomes clear:

Satan says: "To assert control is the only way to be free."

Paul says: "It is for freedom that Christ has set us free. Stand firm, then, and do not let yourselves be burdened again by a yoke of slavery." (Galatians 5:1)

Satan says: "Never let yourself be exploited again!"

Jesus says: "Only the selfless, those who lose themselves completely, will find Me." (see Matthew 10:39)

A word of clarification: Healthy boundaries are a good thing. (It is in part because our perpetrators could not or would not draw healthy boundaries that we went through childhood sexual abuse in the first place.) We are not commanded to roll over and play dead.

What Jesus seems to be saying is this: "Anything you hear about a nonforfeited life is not from Me. I took up the cross and gave up control for the sake of obedience. I am calling you to the same self-denial, not to become someone's doormat but to submit your will to the Father. Only by dying to your sinful and fearful nature will you experience the freedom found in Me."

pause & reflect

1. What control issues have held you in bondage?

2. Personalize the Greatest Lie and the Hardest Truth by putting them in your own words. Rewrite them here.

anger—the unhealthy kind

When was the last time you completely lost it? What was it that made you mad? Did you direct your anger at the right target, or was there a scapegoat caught in the middle? What did the recovery from the outburst look like?

For some of us, these are hard questions. Our self-esteem is so damaged and our sense of worth so shaken that anger becomes a common component in our need for control. This anger can present itself in many ways, some of which paint the bull's-eye on our own foreheads.

Survivors who repress outward anger and turn all those emotions inward think little of their own opinions and their self-worth. Like Karen in chapter 2, they are trapped in the bondage of shame.

Other survivors who attempt to repress anger build impenetrable walls to prevent the possibility of experiencing *any* emotion. Like trying to keep a large beach ball submerged underwater, their attempts to suppress emotion meet with varying degrees of success.

For another group of survivors, repression is not the problem. For them, anger has become a favorite pair of comfortable shoes that can easily be slipped on and off. Anger can be an excellent weapon, and for people who feel the need for control, it can appear to be an effective tool. Why does it seem so effective? There are several reasons:

- *Anger deflects.* When a threat is perceived, anger can be used to help relieve immediate pressure caused by an uncomfortable situation.
- *Anger protects.* Anger can act as a shield, preventing us from unpleasant side effects or consequences such as feeling hurt or humiliated.
- *Anger rationalizes.* By utilizing anger, we not only deflect blame and protect ourselves but we also justify our actions, giving the impression that we're being reasonable.
- *Anger communicates.* Anger is a low-level language, a common denominator through which we can make our point without the bother of exchanging ideas.
- *Anger intimidates.* Anger is often the fastest way to get people to back down. When people defer to us, we get our way and therefore believe we remain in control.

In each case, anger is an indispensable crowbar with which we can pry loose any threats that could topple our carefully constructed house of cards.

anger—the healthy kind

Of course, there are proper expressions of anger. It is perfectly understandable that we are angry about our abuse, angry with our abuser, angry with those who stood by and enabled the abuse to take place, and angry at our sinful reactions to the abuse.

We know from Scripture that not all anger is bad. The Bible records numerous examples of God's wrath: His anger at Israel's repeated rebellion and disbelief; His anger and indignation at Job for presuming to question His methods; Jesus' anger toward the Pharisees, those who desecrated the temple, and Satan (in the Matthew 16 example earlier in this chapter); and most significantly, the full fury of God's wrath at sin poured out on the Savior at the cross.

Anger is an emotion and one of many signs that God has created us in His image. In and of itself, anger is not evil. So where's the line between healthy and unhealthy anger?

The issue is not the presence of the anger but how it is managed. In the biblical examples above, anger was truthfully and graciously expressed. In each instance, the motive behind the anger was love: love for God's chosen people; love for one of Satan's targets (Job); love for the hypocritical Pharisees; love for a disciple (Peter) confused about his Master; and, of course, love for all of humanity for whom Christ gave His life.

The key question is this (you probably saw this one coming): *Does your anger control you?* If the answer is yes, then you've probably crossed the line into unhealthy anger. Anger can provide the illusion of control, but in the end, we need to remember what we discussed in the earlier section about the Greatest Lie: Our quest for control produces our bondage. We cannot only become enslaved to that which we try to control but also that which we *use* to control: anger.

The key is *management*. Paul said, "In your anger do not sin: Do not let the sun go down while you are still angry, and *do not give the devil a foothold*" (Ephesians 4:26-27, emphasis added).

pause & reflect

1. (Survivor), how have you used anger in your relationship? (Spouses), how have you observed the use of anger in your relationship? Compare your honest answers.

2. Where should your anger be directed?

3. How will you hold each other accountable when anger flares?

lighting your own torch

How can we summarize this difficult issue of control? How should we
think of our need to manipulate, especially when contrasted with the

call of the Christian life? Once again, we need look no further than our Savior. Consider Jesus' own testimony from Isaiah:

> The Sovereign LORD has given me an instructed tongue,
>
>> to know the word that sustains the weary.
>
> He wakens me morning by morning,
>
>> wakens my ear to listen like one being taught.
>
> The Sovereign LORD has opened my ears,
>
>> and I have not been rebellious;
>
>> I have not drawn back.
>
> I offered my back to those who beat me,
>
>> my cheeks to those who pulled out my beard;
>
> I did not hide my face
>
>> from mocking and spitting.
>
> Because the Sovereign LORD helps me,
>
>> I will not be disgraced.
>
> Therefore have I set my face like flint,
>
>> and I know I will not be put to shame.
>
> He who vindicates me is near.
>
>> Who then will bring charges against me?
>
>> Let us face each other!
>
> Who is my accuser?
>
>> Let him confront me!
>
> It is the Sovereign LORD who helps me.
>
>> Who is he that will condemn me?

They will all wear out like a garment;

the moths will eat them up. (50:4-9)

He then concludes with a fervent exhortation:

Who among you fears the LORD

and obeys the word of his servant?

Let him who walks in the dark,

who has no light,

trust in the name of the LORD

and rely on his God.

But now, all you who light fires

and provide yourselves with flaming torches,

go, walk in the light of your fires

and of the torches you have set ablaze.

This is what you shall receive from my hand:

You will lie down in torment. (50:10-11)

Who among us does not walk in the dark? Who among us has not been confused, hurt, disappointed, and shamed? Isaiah yielded the floor to the Savior, who — as a Man of Sorrows and acquainted with grief (see Isaiah 53:3) — said, "I know. *I know*. I offered My back, I did not hide My face, but I will not be disgraced; I will not be put to shame; My Vindicator is near. It is the Sovereign Lord who helps Me."

Jesus could have remained in control, righteously and indignantly. But He gave up control, and His enemies will be made a footstool for

His feet (see Psalm 110:1; Hebrews 1:13; 10:13). In the midst of our darkness and humiliation, can we give up control? Or will we light our own torches? To walk in our own light, Jesus said, is the absence of God — it is torment. But then, we already know that, don't we?

becoming accountable

Let the word of Christ dwell in you richly as you teach and
admonish one another with all wisdom, and as you sing psalms,
hymns and spiritual songs with gratitude in your hearts to God.
(Colossians 3:16)

ow for the hard part. But first, let's pause for a minute and
review what we've learned:

- All people, abused or not, are born with a sinful nature and a predisposition to disobey God.
- Because of our confusion, survivors wrongly take on responsibility and shame for the abuse.
- We turn away from intimacy with others because of that shame.
- We seek fulfillment outside of our marriage because of those intimacy issues.
- We isolate ourselves, causing us to keep secrets and relish our victimhood.
- We seek out ways to be in control.

Can you see the progression? Each of these behaviors feeds into
the next. It is a logical pattern that is *very* difficult to break. But we

have laid this pattern next to an extraordinary passage in Colossians 3 and have examined the spiritual effects and remedies the Bible prescribes for the traumatic effects of sin in the world today.

In this chapter's key verse, Colossians 3:16, Paul did not let any of us off the hook — survivor, spouse, bystander, observer. We are charged to "teach and admonish" (instruct and correct) each other because the Word of Christ dwells within us. In other words, we are charged to be accountable to one another. It is this accountability that helps to move us step-by-step into a restored relationship. But like the other challenges we've examined so far, it's not easy.

deconstructing a real-life example

"What on earth are you doing?" The woman's reaction was swift and immediate as she walked into the kitchen and observed her husband pouring milk into a disposable paper cup for their toddler. "She can't drink out of *that!*" she corrected. "It has no lid! Milk will be *everywhere!* What *could* you have been thinking?"

The husband, more than a little dazed, wordlessly walked to the cupboard to find the "right" cup — the one with the lid — and transferred the drink before handing it to the child.

You may have experienced an incident much like this one. While it's easy to decry the mother's overreaction from a distance, this situation is much more complex than it seems. Let's look at this scene through the lens of Christian testimony:

• How should we think of this episode as children of God?

- Despite her past sexual abuse, is the wife called to a different reaction, a different approach, because of her faith in Christ?
- How should the husband have responded? Did he have a choice?
- Consider the child before whom this scene was played out. What did he learn from this situation?

Let's examine this encounter as it relates to each person in the room.

the mother/survivor

You may see the mother's reaction as perfectly legitimate. "Of course she was right to stop what he was doing," you might say. "He should have known better. Can you imagine what might have happened had she *not* intervened? There could have been a terrible mess!" (Survivors *hate* messes.)

As we saw in the last chapter on control, we find it difficult to accept a scenario for which we have not planned all contingencies. But this tendency clashes with the calling of a Christ follower. Let's look to Scripture:

> Do not let any unwholesome talk come out of your mouths, but only what is helpful for building others up according to their needs, that it may benefit those who listen. Get rid of all bitterness, rage and anger, brawling and slander, along with every form of malice. Be kind and compassionate to one another, forgiving each other, just as in Christ God forgave you. (Ephesians 4:29, 31-32)

> My dear brothers, take note of this: Everyone should be quick to
> listen, slow to speak and slow to become angry, for man's anger
> does not bring about the righteous life that God desires. (James
> 1:19-20)

While we may be able to empathize with the mother and perhaps even understand her reaction, as Christians we are called to a
different set of responses.

We may attempt to excuse certain behaviors because of the severity of a trauma and its effects on the victim. We might be tempted to
excuse the ramifications in our own lives as somehow more "understandable." We rationalize by thinking, *Don't I have a right to be given a little slack, considering what I've been through? Can't you have just a little more patience
with me?*

At that point, however, God reminds us of Paul's words to the
Romans:

> For all have sinned and fall short of the glory of God.
> (Romans 3:23)

> So then, each of us will give an account of himself to God.
> (Romans 14:12)

We begin to see that the sins committed against us carry no enti-
tlement. That stands in direct opposition to today's mindset. In
twenty-first-century society, any wrongs or injuries (even perceived

injuries) committed against us immediately demand retribution. It's what keeps the courts packed and the lawyers busy. "Someone needs to pay or be held responsible for what happened," we say, "and it's not going to be me!" Our society has conditioned us to assess blame rather than take responsibility.

Not only have we been taught to assess blame but we've also been taught to assess it according to the severity of the committed act. If a minor traffic accident can produce lasting damage and prompt a litigious response, how much greater is our demand for others' submission and deference when the wounds are deeply physical, psychological, emotional, and spiritual? But we are called to relinquish all claims to special treatment from others — the testimony of a child of God requires it! And we aren't required to be a good Christian witness to only those who are nonbelievers. Consider Paul's convicting words:

> Therefore, as we have opportunity, let us do good to all people, especially to those who belong to the family of believers.
> (Galatians 6:10)

Our witness, Paul said, is critical *within* the household of faith. Indeed, as defined in Paul's analogies of the church as a body, we are each given significant responsibility to set an example for, and minister to, the body of Christ. Essentially, there are no "excuses" that can remove us from accountability.

pause &
reflect

1. Write and then discuss how your actions or behavior may have compromised your testimony both in the church and outside of it.

2. In what ways can you become more accountable to each other as a couple?

the husband/father

Whether the child asked him to help get a drink or he prepared the drink on his own for the child, the husband/father in this scenario was in deep trouble. How could he have reacted to his wife's outburst? There were at least four choices:

- Swallow hard, do as instructed, and say nothing.
- Reflect the anger and tone back to his wife, inciting a full-blown argument.
- Chastise her for the sinful outburst, and, with righteous indignation, demand repentance.
- Respond biblically.

In our example, the husband opted for choice number one. He responded with fear (of confrontation) and assent (to her tone and her treatment).

Many spouses may feel they have no choice in these situations. To return the anger would obviously be wrong, but to make any attempt at discussion or reasoning — even done in the most loving and tactful way — risks a similar reaction, hurt feelings, and an extended recovery period. What to do?

This was a question Jeff frequently asked himself. His wife, an abuse survivor, had a volatile temper and was very demanding. He had learned over the years that the easiest road to harmony in the home was to defer. In the early months of their marriage, this meant voluntarily giving up his desires for hers. Later, it became simple obedience. Finally, it turned into nearly total submission. He saw no way out and the more he gave in, the more she came to expect of him. He had lost himself — he had become almost invisible.

Jeff had repeatedly chosen what he thought was the most harmonious response possible. What he had actually done, however, was enable his wife's demanding behavior. His primary desire to avoid conflict had compromised his witness and encouraged conflict. The family was trapped.

Jesus' dealings tell us much about how to respond biblically to each other. In John 4:1-26 (when Jesus encountered the woman at the well) and again in John 8:1-11 (when He dealt with the woman caught in adultery), we learn key principles for dealing with difficult relationships by observing Him confront unusual behavioral issues. Pause and read those two passages.

Did you notice the way in which Jesus dealt with these women?

- He was not harsh.
- He spoke the truth.
- He lovingly and compassionately reached out.
- He risked misunderstanding and judgment from others.
- He encouraged godly behavior.
- He never once left them in doubt of how much He loved them.

In much the same way, Paul struggled with the Corinthian church, wanting to be honest and truthful as he confronted the church on questionable practices but taking tremendous care to ensure they knew of his abiding love for them:

I am not writing this to shame you, but to warn you, as my dear children. Even though you have ten thousand guardians in Christ, you do not have many fathers, for in Christ Jesus I became your father through the gospel. Therefore I urge you to imitate me. For this reason I am sending to you Timothy, my son whom I love, who is faithful in the Lord. He will remind you of my way of life in Christ Jesus, which agrees with what I teach everywhere in every church. . . . For the kingdom of God is not a matter of talk but of power. What do you prefer? Shall I come to you with a whip, or in love and with a gentle spirit? (1 Corinthians 4:14-17, 20-21)

What an incredible portrait of love and concern! Paul spoke to the Corinthians not as taskmaster or professor but with the love a father would have for his children.

Let's get back to our example. Prior to the situation with the paper cup, Jeff had never risked lovingly and gently confronting his wife's behavior. But suppose he wanted to try. What could he do? There are several approaches he could attempt, depending on the situation and his ability to communicate thoughts and concerns with a loving spirit. Here are three:

Share from a "feeling" level. By stating how his wife's treatment makes him feel, Jeff removes an accusatory tone from his response. He doesn't tell her how sinful her response is but instead says, "I feel . . ." followed by a gentle expression of what it feels like to be the target of her anger. Because feelings are personal and internal, they are less likely targets for a quick counterattack.

Wait until later. Rather than respond in the middle of a volatile situation, it's sometimes best to wait until emotions have cooled. Later, in a more relaxed setting, Jeff could calmly ask to process the earlier event. This waiting period removes Jeff and his wife from the intense, immediate feelings that can be blinding and deafening.

Change the setting. By quietly asking his wife to come into the next room, Jeff could change the "scenery" of the conflict, distancing her from the flash point and allowing emotions to cool.

By employing these methods and following Jesus' guidelines, Jeff could begin to stop the cycle of compliance and start fulfilling the commands to teach and admonish in a loving, gentle, and courageous way. And you could, too.

pause & reflect

Recall one or two recent events that might have compromised your witness. Then discuss the following:

- What triggered the inappropriate response?
- How did you react?
- Who else observed the event, and how were they involved (or not involved) in the subsequent processing of the event?
- What changes (if any) do you need to make to avoid repeating the pattern?

Ask God to change your heart, help you release control, and keep you aware of how your witness affects others.

the child

Children are large, self-propelled sponges. What parent has not been surprised with a repeated word or phrase or an imitated action that the child could only have learned from observation? Self-expression is learned and evolutionary. A small child's first mode of expression is patterned after what others around them say or do.

What did the child in our example learn about mutual respect? How was the biblical instruction to "be quick to listen, slow to speak and slow to become angry" (James 1:19) demonstrated? In our example, the child learned through observation that:

- Daddy is somewhat incapable of caring for me.
- Daddy is not always to be trusted.
- Daddy doesn't deserve my respect or obedience.

If this situation ended without resolution, the child's picture of his parents' relationship would be tainted by these observations and conclusions. If, however, the spouse and survivor are able to deal with the situation right away (without "exploding" or otherwise responding inappropriately), the child will learn valuable lessons about conflict, forgiveness, and grace.

We said earlier that "waiting until later" or "moving to a new setting" might be necessary for spouses dealing with potentially volatile situations. If you need to do this temporarily, please do. But work toward being able to deal with the conflict in real time. Children need to witness the reparation process. If children are shielded from one of the most vital interactions between believers — the requesting and extending of forgiveness and grace — how can we expect them to imitate it?

It is critical that parents become vulnerable not just to each other but, in appropriate measure, to their children as well. Parents who never display weakness, repentance, or submission in front of children portray an incomplete picture of what it means to be a child of God. This incomplete picture is at odds with the Bible's call for authenticity in Christian witness and the testimony of our faith.

super-spirituality versus authenticity

Let's go a little deeper with this issue of authenticity. Many survivors are superb performers. Because they are careful to avoid being seen as damaged or vulnerable, survivors can assume an air of "super-spirituality." They want to appear to be the most "together," most complete, most involved, most spiritual Christians in their churches. Survivors will often be the first to volunteer when ministry opportunities arise. They also happily and freely dispense advice and counsel to others despite significant unresolved issues in their own lives. While in part they do these things out of their love for Christ, they may also do them to deflect attention from their own personal issues.

This facade is practiced not only by survivors but also by their spouses, particularly when they are together. They keep up appearances because they feel it's expected of them. It's possible they haven't been exposed to an open and honest body of believers, where they would soon realize they are not alone in their struggles.

Herein lies the power of community. At our church, Cheryl and I work with groups of survivors as well as separately with just survivors and their spouses. Without a doubt, the most powerful and life-changing moments occur when Christians come together and become vulnerable with each other. When survivors and spouses discover that a wounded community exists in their midst, they realize there is no need for masks. This is often a dramatic moment, and one that produces something survivors have rarely felt: freedom. Freedom from pretense, freedom from bondage to the past, freedom from the pressure to perform, and freedom from a witness that they wish were more genuine. Jesus said, "The truth will set you free" (John 8:32). Indeed, freedom in Christ can strip off the masks and open the doors to authenticity and vulnerability.

the modeling effect

Most couples, whether affected by sexual abuse or not, resolve to avoid making as many mistakes as their parents. They determine they will not continue poor patterns modeled by parents or other adults of influence. They soon discover that this plan is easier said than done, and many learn that the more widespread the dysfunction, the harder it is to guard against.

Consider this list of characteristics attributed to sexual abuse perpetrators:

- Emotionally ill
- No appropriate emotional expression
- No self-control

- Self-pitying
- Self-absorbed
- No boundaries
- Controlled by fear
- Need to dominate and control their environment

These characteristics manifest themselves in very specific destructive ways in perpetrators. As a survivor, you have borne the brunt of the effects of those actions. Now look at the list again. Do any of those behaviors ring *another* bell? As a survivor, do you find yourself exhibiting variations of these traits in your current family situation? Consider the chart below and see if any of the characteristics in the right-hand column apply to you:

PERPETRATORS	SURVIVORS
Emotionally ill	Emotionally insecure
No appropriate emotional expression	Unable to express emotional needs
No self-control	Poor impulse control
Self-absorbed	Low self-esteem
No boundaries	Unable to set appropriate boundaries
Driven by fear	Driven by fear
Need to control	Need to control

If this looks familiar, you are not alone. Many survivors are determined to stop the cycle of abuse. But try as they might, they find themselves falling into the same traps and behaviors from which they had originally suffered. These behaviors may be packaged differently, but the effects are similarly destructive. Survivors have a need for ongoing sympathy and continual reassurance, an inability to set limits on themselves, and no healthy model after which to pattern their self-expression.

Cheryl's experiences with her father are a perfect example of this effect. He was a bootlegger and drug dealer who went to prison three times for armed robbery and forgery. One afternoon, Cheryl got into a fistfight with a classmate while defending her younger sister. The fight began right outside their home, and in the heat of the battle, her father walked outside to investigate the commotion. The crowd that had gathered to watch the fight parted and became silent as he approached. As the girls stopped fighting to look up at him, he knelt down and said to Cheryl, "You finish this here and now, or when you come inside, I'll finish you." (Actually, more colorful language was used.) Then he calmly walked back inside.

Cheryl's father had done exactly what he thought he should do: prepare his children to make their own way in a hard and difficult world. But the example had been set. Later, she would repeat that behavior in her own life. Remember Cheryl's story? At fifteen she married to escape her home situation. As her marriage progressed, her husband became verbally and then physically abusive. One of the main reasons for the escalation to physical abuse was because Cheryl was taught to "give as good as she got." Once the physical abuse started, the fights between them became more and more violent.

To the list of long-term effects of sexual abuse, we must add a propensity to carry forward, in some fashion, the same characteristics that so debilitated us.

a new beginning

However, we can't leave this section without making one thing clear: This cycle can be stopped. As we discussed in chapter 2, many survivors assume shame that is not theirs to own. We must put the blame for the abuse squarely where it lies: on the perpetrator and ultimately on the Deceiver himself, Satan.

It's hard to admit that our abuse has caused us to make bad decisions, react out of fear, and even take on the behavior patterns of the abuser. But it's not hard to see *why* that happens. It's what we saw, what we knew, what we came to expect, and, in many ways, how we protected ourselves.

But there is hope. Look at Jesus' words:

> "He who has an ear, let him hear what the Spirit says to the churches. To him who overcomes, I will give some of the hidden manna. I will also give him a white stone with a new name written on it, known only to him who receives it." (Revelation 2:17)

What tapes have been playing in the back of your mind? What names have you called yourself? Christ says that overcomers have a new name. And here's the best part, from 1 John 5:5: "Who is it that overcomes the world? Only he who believes that Jesus is the Son of God."

He has a new name for you. Stop calling yourself "weak," "loser," "failure," or "hopeless." Just imagine the private, personal, sacred name Christ has waiting for you. Maybe it's on the order of "beloved" or "adored." Perhaps it has the ring of "redeemed" or "forgiven" or "cherished." This new name is part of an inheritance reserved in heaven for you (see 1 Peter 1:4), and it's given to you because "if anyone is in Christ, he is a new creation" (2 Corinthians 5:17).

This is why the cycle can be stopped. This is why there is hope that the patterns of behavior you've seen, experienced, and maybe even practiced can be discarded. You were bought at a price; given a new, private, holy name; and supernaturally made new — not by your own power but by His.

pause & reflect

1. (Survivor), which of the perpetrator characteristics were evident in the person (or people) who abused you? Which have you adopted into your current behaviors? Share these with your spouse.

2. What would it take for you as a couple to hold each other accountable for these behaviors?

3. What aspect of the sinful nature has been hardest to overcome in your married life?

4. Do you sometimes play to each other's weaknesses? If so, why do you think that occurs? How can you put an end to this kind of behavior?

5. What "new name" do you imagine Christ has given you? How does it feel to be given such a name?

thankfulness

The last element we want to deal with in the discussion of accountability and witness is thankfulness. How, you may ask, is the issue of being thankful related to the testimony of Christ in our lives? It is significant that Paul discusses thankfulness in the key verses of this and the previous chapter. Look again at these verses:

> Let the peace of Christ rule in your hearts, since as members of one body you were called to peace. And be thankful. Let the word of Christ dwell in you richly as you teach and admonish one another with all wisdom, and as you sing psalms, hymns and spiritual songs with gratitude in your hearts to God.
> (Colossians 3:15-16)

Our ability to experience peace, give up control, and cultivate a witness that honors Christ is in large part dependent on our ability to be thankful. Remember our discussion in chapter 3 of Jesus' parable about the unforgiving servant? The servant's inability to be thankful and appreciate his own pardon fueled the harsh treatment he showed his own debtor.

In the same way, our capacity to teach and admonish each other in a spirit of gentleness and humility can be done only through an attitude of thankfulness, not an attitude of superiority or puffed-up knowledge. It's an "attitude of gratitude."

John's first epistle expresses a thankful heart:

How great is the love the Father has lavished on us, that we should be called children of God! And that is what we are! (1 John 3:1)

We love because he first loved us. (1 John 4:19)

Our initial acceptance of God's love, our ongoing process of becoming Christlike, and our testimony to the body of Christ and the world compel us to respond with gratitude for God's grace.

There is an added benefit of thankfulness: Reveling in our Christ-defined identity dismantles our demand for entitlements and points us instead to the freeing truth that God sees us as infinitely valuable. That same thankfulness helps strengthen our witness as we embrace the surpassing love of the God who would purchase and redeem us at so high a cost.

May God grant that our testimony to His love be authentic and compassionate.

pause & reflect   Make a list together of the things for which you are thankful. Then pray through the list together, praising God for His goodness and thanking Him for His generosity.

rediscovering sexual intimacy

Now for the *really* hard part.

epidemic proportions

We've finished our examination of a compelling Colossians passage, and we pray that the Spirit will commit us to the truths we've studied. Anything else? Well, yes. There's one more subject on which we need to shed light. This one needs purification, it needs to go through detox, and, to make matters worse, we'd rather not talk about it — certainly not in church.

Many Christian couples have been happily married for years and have never discussed it. The problem is, that's exactly what the Enemy wants us to do. Satan is perfectly happy when the church ignores the issue of sexual intimacy. He prefers that we pretend the problem doesn't exist. In this way he perpetuates the dysfunction. Consider:

> Any disease unexposed and unaddressed is by definition an
> epidemic because there is no containment effort.

Unabated and unchecked, unwillingness to deal with problems associated with sexual intimacy morphs and reproduces. Like a virulent disease, the unwillingness adapts and finds new ways to persist.

what it looks like

What are the effects of abuse on sexual intimacy? Here are a few examples:

- Julia can endure sex with her husband — but only in total darkness with her face covered.
- Necking and snuggling are okay, but Colleen shuts down at the first sign of sensual stimulation or pleasure; she cannot receive it. Because she felt pleasure as a ten-year-old during her brother's abuse, any sexual pleasure now feels wrong.
- Sex for Kate must be planned far in advance and completed in a strict, almost regimental procedure. There is no deviation from the plan and no spontaneity. Kate believes that if sex is made as perfunctory as possible, she won't have to engage her feelings and she won't be hurt again.
- When her husband starts getting excited during sex, Erica leaves the room mentally, just as she did during her father's nighttime visits. She "returns" just in time to fake an orgasm for the benefit of her husband. She hasn't actually had one since long before her marriage.

what it's really about

In dealing with these encounters, many couples believe the biggest problem is the sexual act itself. That's usually not the real problem. You may have heard the saying "Sex is 90 percent mental, 10 percent physical." In many ways, this is true. But a truer saying might be this: "God made sex to be 100 percent spiritual."

Biblically defined, sex is a physical manifestation of a spiritual union. God has ordained many different expressions of spiritual unions:

- Love one another (John 13:34).
- Encourage one another (1 Thessalonians 5:11).
- Serve one another (Galatians 5:13).
- Submit to one another (Ephesians 5:21).
- Accept one another (Romans 15:7).
- Be devoted to one another (Romans 12:10).
- Honor one another (Romans 12:10).

The marriage relationship is special among all spiritual unions. It is so special that God exalted it in an unparalleled way. What God says, in effect, is this:

"I took the two of you and made you one. *I did that*. You can't undo it. In the acts of betrothal, commitment, and marriage, I supernaturally joined the two of you together in a mysterious, almost unexplainable way. This union is the most intimate expression of community that is possible on earth and, in fact, is so holy, so sacred that it is built on the same model as my Son and His bride: the church. There is nothing Christ has withheld from His beloved church; there is nothing she, as His bride, should withhold from Him. This is your template."

Sex is a deep, physical, marriage-based expression of the loving, serving, accepting, and honoring all Christians are called to do. It goes beyond these actions, however, and takes them to a new level in the most intimate of spiritual unions.

The problem is that the world has taken that manifestation and infected it. Paul addressed this issue when he wrote,

Flee from sexual immorality. All other sins a man commits are outside his body, but he who sins sexually sins against his own body. Do you not know that your body is a temple of the Holy Spirit, who is in you, whom you have received from God? You are not your own; you were bought at a price. Therefore honor God with your body. (1 Corinthians 6:18-20)

It is by God's design that as the single greatest expression of intimacy between humans, sex is saved for last. Prior to marriage, couples are encouraged to intentionally build social, emotional, and spiritual bonds. The most vulnerable and fragile bond is saved for last. And while respect for the fragility of sex is rarely seen today, it is not because God doesn't command it.

So what's intimacy really about? It may seem like it's about nakedness, embarrassment, or specific sexual acts. It's not. It's about *vulnerability*.

Let's consider for a moment the surrender of heart required to become a follower of Christ. When believers choose to trust Christ for their salvation, they come to the following conclusions, stated here in the first person:

I had to reach a point of defenselessness to accept and receive Christ as Savior. I had to give myself over to Him fully in order for Him to save me, complete me, and make me whole. In the words of the old hymn, He had "broken every barrier down." I had to trust that Jesus desires only good for me. I had to be open to seeing the love He has expressed for me in order to give everything to Him.

The same openness must exist in that most sacred and *most representative* earthly relationship: our marriage. In the same spirit we came to Christ, we should desire to say to our spouse:

I believe God has given you to me. My defenses are down because I accept you, receive you, and trust you. I will try to give myself to you fully so you can complete me and make me whole. I will remove all barriers. I know you want only good for me. I will open myself to give everything I am to you.

Can you see the parallels? It's the same spirit of vulnerability. This is why Paul wrote in Ephesians,

> Husbands, love your wives, just as Christ loved the church and
> gave himself up for her. . . . In this same way, husbands ought to
> love their wives as their own bodies. He who loves his wife loves
> himself. (5:25,28)

**pause &
reflect**   Repeat to each other the paragraph on the previous page that represents a commitment made to Christ. Then read the paragraph that represents a commitment made to a spouse. Perhaps you'd like to personalize this by repeating your wedding vows. Ask God to help you release your fears and increase your trust in one another.

Review these expressions of spiritual unions:

- Love one another.
- Encourage one another.
- Serve one another.
- Submit to one another.
- Accept one another.
- Be devoted to one another.
- Honor one another.

For each one, commit to an action step that will take you and your spouse to a deeper level of emotional intimacy. This is an important step toward God-honoring sexual intimacy.

dancing in the dark

As we've discussed, couples dealing with childhood sexual abuse frequently have problems communicating with each other on a wide range of subjects. This is particularly evident with the subject of sexuality. This inability to talk openly about sex is further crippled by the coping mechanisms we sometimes employ. Consider some of the more frequent aftereffects.

in the survivor

Loss of sexual desire. Because of the past perversion, sexual intimacy is shunned and avoided. And because sensations of pleasure may have been felt during the abuse, pleasure becomes inextricably linked with guilt and shame. Sexual stimulation stops being a gift from God and instead becomes what Satan desires it to be: a source of pain and isolation.

Promiscuity. After the abuse, some survivors become scavengers in search of the "right" or "perfect" sexual experience. They may also become perpetrators themselves, exacting revenge by toying with emotions and then dashing expectations. This can produce tremendous guilt and an inability to accept forgiveness.

Homosexual feelings or experimentation. It's not surprising that survivors often seek solace from members of the same sex. The Enemy can pollute this process as well by transforming feelings of comfort and safety into the desire for physical intimacy with same-sex friends who provide consolation. Because historically the church hasn't dealt well with such sensitive matters, the homosexual feelings can produce oppressive shame. Often survivors who experience these feelings believe there is no one with whom they can share this burden.

Substitution. A preoccupation with pornography can become a substitute for intimacy in a marriage. This is tempting for survivors because it keeps *real* human contact at a minimum.

in the spouse

Gravitation toward pornography. Because a couple's sexual experience may be limited in scope and infrequent in practice, spouses sometimes seek sexual fulfillment in pornographic magazines, at "gentleman's clubs," or through the Internet via picture or movie downloads or participation in sex-themed chat rooms (which could also fit under the category of "Extramarital Affairs").

Excessive masturbation. While the appropriateness of masturbation is a matter of some disagreement and controversy, few would argue that taken to an extreme, it is unhealthy. It can sap sexual energy that should be reserved for the marriage or even become preferential to sexual activity with a spouse.

Extramarital affairs. Rationalizations abound for seeking gratification outside the marriage relationship. While often prompted by an infrequent and mechanical sexual relationship in the marriage, it is clearly not an acceptable behavior. Of course the central irony of extramarital affairs is that when people seek fulfillment and completeness outside the marriage, their sexual experience instead becomes vacant and empty. Instead of an act bonding two people closer together, it becomes an act of separation tainted with guilt and hidden by secrecy.

God wants couples to be healed from these consequences and be equipped to minister to each other, but this is possible only through open communication and dialogue. The stigma of the subject must be removed. Sex must no longer be an "elephant in the room" we can't discuss. We must stop reducing sex to something that is merely endured.

Consider God's Word on the subject of sex:

> Be faithful to your own wife.
>
>   She is like your own well of water from which you drink. . . .
>
> Be happy with the wife
>
>   you married when you were young.
>
> She gives you joys
>
>   as your fountain gives you water.
>
> She is as lovely and graceful as a deer.
>
>   Let her love always make you happy.
>
>   Let her love always hold you captive.
>
>   (Proverbs 5:15,18-19, NCV)

> Drink and imbibe deeply, O lovers. (Song of Solomon 5:1, NASB)

God not only created sex but He also blessed it in a marriage relationship. In the Song of Solomon, God glorified the sexual experience, opening a window into seductive conversations and scenes between Solomon and his bride. An in-depth study of this book might surprise Christians who, in an effort to distance themselves from *anything* that might resemble our often-profane culture, have abandoned a biblical approach to physical intimacy in marriage.

For female survivors and their spouses, we highly recommend the book *Intimate Issues*,[5] by Linda Dillow and Lorraine Pintus, for a frank, honest, and biblical treatment of sexual intimacy in marriage. The book includes a chapter that speaks directly to those who have suffered sexual abuse.

pause & reflect

Together, pray again that God will deepen the sexual experience between the two of you. Do not be afraid to take this request to Him — He desires your fulfillment in His perfect design!

Take a step toward deeper intimacy by giving each other permission to express fears and hopes of intimacy. It will not be easy, but God will honor your efforts to bond your relationship closer together. Set aside enough time for both of you to share, and choose a safe, quiet setting that won't be threatened by interruption.

the real objective

The ultimate objective of all Christ followers is to bring glory to God in response to His astonishing love for us. Have you considered that an excellent way to glorify and honor God is to enjoy the wonderful craftsmanship of both your physical bodies? Here are a few action steps you can take now to glorify God in your physical intimacy and significantly deepen your relationship:

Pray. Jesus said, "Ask and it will be given to you; seek and you will find; knock and the door will be opened to you. For everyone who asks receives" (Matthew 7:7-8). James 4:2 tells us, "You do not have, because you do not ask God." How blessed we are that we can ask the Architect of our physical bodies to help us in the most intimate expression of love He has given us! If you've never prayed for God to help you open your hearts to each other, expose the lies of the Enemy, and make the most of His extravagant gift of sex, start today.

Communicate. As we've said before, Satan is a big fan of silence. He has successfully suppressed sexual dialogue in our marriages and churches, in part by convincing us that if we talk about it, we cheapen it. But this is true only if we use the world's vocabulary and the world's context to do so. Tell each other your desires, fears, and dreams. How?

- Affirm your love for each other and your desire to express it.
- Confess that it's awkward to talk about these things but that you want to try.
- Stop and pray, asking God to give you the words.
- Ask for your spouse's help in starting the conversation.
- Affirm your faith that God will honor your request.

Be intentional. We sometimes assume we'll figure it out as we go but then don't take any concrete steps to begin the process. You might consider purchasing a book on sexual intimacy that is written from a Christian perspective. Seek a trusted friend who will pray for you and be on the lookout for additional resources. Set aside time for yourselves away from distractions. Time spent together, even without the expectation of sex, will deepen the relationship between you and draw you closer for when you do have an opportunity to express sexual intimacy.

summary

Many people in churches today suffer the scars of childhood sexual abuse and feel they have nowhere to turn, no safe place of refuge, and no one to understand. This book was written to encourage couples to begin a dialogue, seek understanding from each other, and trust in the God of all comfort to honor their desire for wholeness.

Please pray with us as we reflect on our study, God's instruction from His Word, and how the Spirit has moved in our hearts:

Lord of light and life, Lover of our souls, we are compelled to worship You for Your relentless pursuit of us, even in our despair and doubt. We honor You in the only ways we know how: half-hearted and halting, unsure and unsteady, but with hope for a remade heart through the redemption and deliverance offered at the Cross.

Create in us a heart made whole by a Savior intimately familiar with sorrow and grief—a fellow traveler, victim, survivor, and conqueror. Restore us from shame, bring intimacy to our relationships, complete us through each other, grant us peace, and make us accountable. Defeat us where pride, defensiveness, or embarrassment would keep us from openness and vulnerability. And in our brokenness, bring us a taste of the joy You have prepared for us before the foundation of the world. Amen.

notes

1. Jim Hopper, "Child Abuse: Statistics, Research, and Resources" (Boston University School of Medicine, 1998), www.jimhopper.com/abstats/#s-sources, www.darkness2light.org/KnowAbout/statistics.shtml (accessed May 6, 2004).
2. Robert S. McGee and Dr. Harry Schaumburg, *Renew: Hope for Victims of Sexual Abuse* (Houston: Rapha Publishing, 1990), p. 5.
3. Frederick Buechner, *Wishful Thinking: A Theological ABC* (San Francisco: Harper and Row, 1973), p. 24.
4. C. S. Lewis, *The Great Divorce* (San Francisco: HarperSanFrancisco, 2001).
5. Linda Dillow and Lorraine Pintus, *Intimate Issues: 21 Questions Christian Women Ask About Sex* (Colorado Springs, Colo.: WaterBrook, 1999).

about the authors

brad and Cheryl Tuggle live in San Antonio, Texas, where Brad is a minister at the Oak Hills Church. Brad is a former businessman of twenty years who now ministers full-time in the areas of discipleship and abuse recovery. Being asked to share Cheryl's story of abuse and the struggle in their marriage uncovered a groundswell to begin a dialogue in the church about this sensitive but pervasive subject.

Their ministry also involves ongoing support groups and counseling to sexual abuse survivors and their spouses. Brad and Cheryl have been interviewed several times on *Renewal*, a daily radio broadcast sponsored by Fellowship Bible Church North and Dr. Gene Getz.

Cheryl enjoys gardening and cooking, and Brad is a runner who plays golf when he can. They have two daughters, Catherine and Victoria.

FIND OUT WHERE TRUE CHANGE BEGINS AND HOW TO ACHIEVE IT.

The Wounded Heart

Dr. Allender's book explores the secret lament of the soul damaged by sexual abuse and lays hold of the hope buried there by the One whose unstained image we all bear.

Dr. Dan B. Allender   0-89109-289-7

Inside Out

Spiritual growth involves change—becoming more like Christ and less like our old selves. If you want a more vital union with God, richer relationships, and a deeper sense of wholeness, *Inside Out* is a great place to start.

Dr. Larry Crabb   1-57683-082-9

To order copies, visit your local Christian bookstore, call NavPress at 1-800-366-7788, or log on to www.navpress.com.

To locate a Christian bookstore near you, call 1-800-991-7747.

BRINGING TRUTH TO LIFE
www.navpress.com